Jesus Was Adopted

Triumph of the Human Spirit from the Lives of
Celebrated People Who Were Adopted

Gregory P. Hawkins

EPIPHANY
PUBLISHING

2012

Published in the United States of America by:

Epiphany Publishing Company
10714 S. Jordan Gateway, Suite 100
South Jordan, Utah 84095

www.epiphanypublishingcompany.com

ISBN 978-0-9849528-0-9

Library of Congress Control Number: 2012930359

Cover design by J.P. Hawkins
Interior artwork images by Sterling Morris
Cover photo by Jessica Tenney

This book is dedicated to the children.

Table of Contents

Introduction to Parents

When we adopted our daughter Elizabeth, I was asked an interesting question by the press. Elizabeth was a teenager and had spent nearly a decade in the foster care system of our state. She was considered by the state to be *at risk* educationally and *special needs* for the purpose of adoption. This was primarily because of her age and her long tenure in foster care, not because she had any disabilities or because she was academically challenged—she was not.

I was asked how we intended to deal with her special needs. I answered, "The same way we deal with all of our children's special needs." I then told the reporter that, "I have never met a teenager who wasn't *at risk* or who didn't have *special needs.*"

I still hold to that answer—mostly.

My perspective, however, has come into clearer focus. After long experience, I have come to know that those "normal" and "usual" issues with which most teenagers deal are more acutely felt by adopted teenagers. More importantly, these issues are aggravated by other serious questions.

For the purpose of this book, I am using the

term *adopted* loosely to mean being raised, in part or in whole, without one or both biological parents.

Most adopted teens, at some level, are grateful for family, grateful to be *adopted*. Still, they deal directly with the issue of identity. Because they do not know one or both of their parents or significant parts of their ancestry, the timeless questions of life take on special importance: *Who am I? Where did I come from? Where am I going?*

The secondary questions are even more poignant: *How will my family's past, which I don't even know, affect my future? Why was I placed for adoption? Is there something wrong with me? Is my adopted family going to last?*

Adopted teenagers feel that they are different. More to the point, they think that everyone around them can obviously see that they are different. And, even when the feelings of rejection and abandonment diminish and become manageable with time, scars can remain for a lifetime. Add to these gnawing feelings of rejection and abandonment, the awful tragedy—for both parent and teen—of diminished attachment.

This book is not intended as a manual or guide to help parents meet the very real needs of their adopted teenagers whom they love so dearly.

It is, rather, to directly help the teenager move from looking down in fear, anxiety, and discouragement, to looking forward with hope, anticipation, and possibility.

As I have shared these stories of celebrated adopted people who have achieved some measure of accomplishment, I have seen a light turn on. Hope has been born. Thought has been stimulated. Purpose has been strengthened.

As a lawyer who has worked with hundreds of adoptive parents, as a teacher who has taught thousands of teenagers and as a parent of four adopted children and two step-children, I am acutely aware of the very real challenges that face you and your children. I have also been privileged to experience, as have you, the absolute joy of being part of a teenager's life.

I offer this book as a small token of help and hope.

Forward

Dear Friend,

This book is for you. It contains part of the story of many very special people. All people have value. All people have a story. All people have dreams and feel pain. The people in this book share something special and unique with you and with me.

I hope you will begin to look closely at your life and see the possibilities. Truly, the possibilities for your future are unnumbered and unimaginable. You are the writer of your own story. To be sure, there are many participants. But, it is your story.

The men and women you will read about are not really different from you. Each of us, me, you and them, share one thing very unique and important.

I was adopted; you were adopted; they were adopted.

With hope and confidence,

Your Friend

Dave Thomas

Founder, Wendy's
Old Fashioned Hamburgers

(July 2, 1932 – January 8, 2002)

Dave Thomas

"Thomas's adoptive father remarried three times, so Dave
was bounced around a lot from home to home. In his
biography, Dave's Way, Thomas say these childhood traumas
taught him some important lessons that helped him become
successful in business. These lessons were:

1. Look for people who care about you, and learn from
   them.
2. Dream early, and build your goals on your dream.
3. Learn to rely on yourself early.
4. If there are things you don't like in the world you
   grow up in, make your own world different.
5. Take a step every day.
6. Be yourself." *(p.76)*

*Taken from The Young Entrepreneur's Guide to Starting and Running a
Business by Steve Mariotti, Debra DeSalvo, Tony Towle, Random House
Digital, Inc. New York, Second Edition published in 2000.*

Sixty years old and comfortable with a life well
lived, Dave Thomas stared out through the window.
But his eyes took little notice of the Florida sunlight
reflecting off the water behind his Fort Lauderdale
home. Instead, his mental gaze was directed inward.
Something disturbed the quiet of his mind, an error
he had made with the best of intentions when he was
a very young man.

As soon as he got his first job in a restaurant when

he was only 12 years old, Dave Thomas knew where he wanted to work for the rest of his life. He loved restaurant work. He quit high school to pursue his dream when he was 15. Now, that decision had come back to haunt him. He had been successful — wildly so, — but what would his example say to teenagers now? What would his legacy be? He was troubled by his decision to quit high school.

Even this late in life, he could imagine only one solution to the problem. Thomas had never been afraid of work. He wasn't afraid now. He would go back to school and work to change that decision. In 1992 he enrolled in school, and a year later graduated from Coconut Creek High School with a GED. With a twinkle in his eye and an inward chuckle he accepted another award, his classmates' voted that he was "most likely to succeed."

Dave Thomas had started life in somewhat difficult circumstances. He was born during the Great Depression, on July 2, 1932, in Atlantic City, New Jersey. His mother gave him up and at six weeks of age, he was adopted by Rex and Auleva Thomas. The Thomases were good to him but when he was five he and his family suffered the death of Auleva Thomas. His father, Rex, like a lot of other men during that time, had trouble getting or keeping work. They drifted from job to job around the country.

One thing about this time stood out for Dave: summers at his grandmother's house in Michigan. Minnie Sinclair, his grandmother, taught him a lot when she had him in her home. She showed him what it felt like to serve others, to treat everybody with respect, to make and keep friends, to be successful in his relationships with other people.

When Dave was 12, that first job that showed him his true calling in life was at a restaurant in Knoxville, Tennessee, called The Regas. It didn't last long, but the good impression he made on some of the people there lasted many years, and the happy impact of the job on him lasted a lifetime.

When Dave was 15, his father had a job in Ft. Wayne, Indiana. Dave found a job as a busboy at the Hobby House, a restaurant whose owner proved to be a great mentor in Dave's life. When Dave's father needed to move to find another job, Dave decided not to go with him but to quit school and work full time. He moved into the YMCA. He was happy in his work, and his bosses were happy with him.

When Dave Thomas was 18, the Korean War had begun. Fearing being drafted into the infantry, he decided to enlist so that he would be able to have some input on where he ended up. The Army sent him to Fort Benning, Georgia, where he was enrolled at the Cook's and Baker's School. When he finished his training, he was posted to Germany where he fed 2,000 soldiers a day. He later attributed some of his successful innovations in the fast-food industry to his experiences as a mess sergeant in the Army.

At the age of 21, honorably discharged with the rank of Staff Sergeant, he returned to Indiana and to the Hobby House restaurant. He became the head cook. While working there, he met Colonel Harland Sanders, the founder of Kentucky Fried Chicken (KFC). The Colonel would soon have a great influence on his life. Colonel Sanders convinced Thomas's bosses to change their restaurant over to his KFC franchise. They bought up other KFC franchise restaurants..

When Thomas was 30, his bosses asked him to take over four of their KFC restaurants in Columbus, Ohio, that were failing. In four years Thomas had managed to turn them around and make them profitable. When he sold them back to KFC, his commission made him a millionaire.

Money in hand, Thomas set about making the dream that had grown inside him come true, of opening a hamburger restaurant that would be different from all the others. He wanted a place where sandwiches were made as ordered by the customer, not made in advance and kept limply warm under a heat lamp. He wanted a family restaurant with a comfortable, homelike environment.

He opened his first restaurant, naming it Wendy's Old Fashioned Hamburgers, with carpeted floors and old-fashioned-looking furnishings. The hamburgers, instead of being frozen and round, were fresh and square to emphasize one of Thomas' guiding principles — don't cut corners. Drawing upon his Army experiences and using his creativity, he developed the first pick-up window, the first salad bar and the sale of baked potatoes as a fast-food option.

Dave Thomas received every major award offered by his industry and was honored as a pioneer. He ascribed his secret of success to those lessons taught him long before by his grandmother. His own loyalty to the values of service, respect and hard work translated into customer loyalty. He gave value and the customers showed their appreciation by giving him success beyond his dreams.

He became well known in his later years by appearing in over 800 commercials over the 13-year span that he served as the voice and face of Wendy's Restaurants. Developing a down-to-earth, honest, and comfortable style, he was a surprising success in advertising, even earning recognition in the Guinness Book of World Records for the length of the television advertising campaign that featured him as its star.

Despite all his success and all the recognition and awards, Dave Thomas stayed true to his humble beginnings. He always said he was just a hamburger cook. Whether it was friends, employees, or mere acquaintances, everybody who knew him spoke of him as one of the good guys. Truly this was one nice guy who did not finish last.

His life mirrored the vastly popular stories of the 19th-century novelist Horatio Alger Jr., who gained literary fame for his tales of disadvantaged young boys who grew up to achieve great success and the fulfillment of the American dream. Like the characters in the stories, Thomas reached his goals through hard work, courage and determination. In 1979, he received the Horatio Alger Award for his life's work.

Thomas believed that with great success came great responsibility. Among the many contributions of time and money he made in his life, one of the most important to him was the Dave Thomas Foundation for Adoption. Having been adopted himself, he wanted the same permanence and love he had felt as a child for every child in similar circumstances.

In line with this goal, Thomas was honored to be appointed as the head of the White House Initiative on Adoption in 1990. He spent countless hours working toward making adoptions easier for all families involved. His work resulted in many corporations making adoption part of their corporate benefits packages. He campaigned for two ground-breaking adoption laws. In 1996, the United States enacted a law to allow adoptive parents a tax break when they adopt a child. Thomas was instrumental in getting another law passed by Congress in 1997 to speed up the process of adoption.

He lived in Florida at the end of his life, still giving and still working behind the scenes to make good things happen for other people as they had happened for him. He considered his family his greatest success, even greater than the fact that there were over 6,000 Wendy's Restaurants in service. He died at his home in Fort Lauderdale, Florida, on January 8, 2002, happy in a life well lived.

Frederick Douglass

Slave, Orator, Writer,
Statesman and Social Reformer
(February, 1818 – February 20, 1895)

Frederick Douglass

"If nothing is expected of a people, that people will find it difficult to contradict that expectation." *(p. 25)*

Quoted from the speech WHAT THE BLACK MAN WANTS –
Delivered to The Massachusetts Anti-Slavery Society at Boston. From The
Selected Addresses of Frederick Douglass – An African American Heritage
Book. By Frederick Douglass – (2008, Wilder Publications, LLC; Radford
Virginia).

"Oh! Had I the ability, and could I reach the nation's ear, I would today pour out a fiery stream of biting ridicule, blasting reproach, withering sarcasm, and stern rebuke. For it is not light that is needed, but fire; it is not the gentle shower, but thunder. We need the storm, the whirlwind, and the earthquake."

Frederick Douglass, p. 691 – The Essential Frederick Douglas taken from
THE HYPOCRISY OF AMERICAN SLAVERY – Delivered in
Rochester, New York, July 4, 1852. 2008 Wilder Publications.

The flow of people moved like an incoming tide, down the streets and alleys from every direction, mostly on foot. Only those with the highest status and money traveled by carriage. Nearing their destination, they spoke in hushed tones but with some excitement. The evening promised an unusual entertainment.

The date was October 14, 1845, in the city of Cork, near the southern coast of Ireland.

As the gathering of spectators began to fill the meeting hall, the air grew warm, the atmosphere thick and airless. Many fidgeted in their seats. Most had never seen a black man, let alone an escaped American slave, one with a bounty on his head.

The United Kingdom had abolished the slave trade in 1807 and finally freed all its slaves by 1833. Yet in the days of slavery in the British Empire, the majority of African slaves were transported to its colonies, especially the West Indies; relatively few were brought to the British Isles.

The citizens of England, Scotland, and Ireland abhorred the concept of slavery. Still, the audience wondered how a man without any formal education and raised in bondage would act and dress. Some could not help but speculate whether he would address the audience in complete English sentences or speak in a savage tongue that required a translator.

The local newspaper, *The Cork Examiner,* reported that the 27-year-old Douglass dressed and spoke "with the ease and grace of a gentleman—a gentleman of nature and society. . . . His voice is well toned and musical, . . . and his manner easy and graceful."

Frederick Douglass held his audience spellbound. He told them that as a slave he was considered little more than a beast. "I was the same as a chattel, a thing of household property, to be bought and sold, or used according to the will of my master," he told them. "I was subject to all the evils and horrors of slavery—to the lash, the chain, the thumb-screw; and even as I stand here before you I bear on my back the marks of the lash."

That very evening as he spoke to the people in the hall, slave hunters continued their legally sanctioned search back in the United States, to find and return him to his master and owner. Although he and his family lived in the free state of Massachusetts, the law of the land allowed the slave states to track him down anywhere in the nation.

Four years before he began his speaking tour of Great Britain, he traveled throughout the northern free states, lecturing and writing about the evils of slavery.

He placed himself in extreme danger by publishing his autobiography, *The Narrative of the Life of Frederick Douglass, An American Slave, Written by Himself.* The book became an instant bestseller. It so infuriated the slave-owning society that Douglass was forced to flee to Britain for his safety.

He was born Frederick Bailey in February 1818 to Harriet Bailey, a field slave frequently rented to other farmers. His father was rumored to be Captain Aaron Anthony, who claimed Frederick as property. Captain Anthony managed the extensive plantations of a man named Colonel Lloyd. Rarely seeing his mother, Frederick was placed with his grandmother, Betsey. His mother died when he was seven or eight, but no one told him about her death at the time.

When Frederick was six, his grandmother prepared them both for a journey to see the "Old Master" at the

Lloyd Plantation, meaning Colonel Lloyd. Affected by her obvious fear, he clung to her skirt for most of the trip. Upon arrival at the elegant mansion, she left him outside to play. He never saw her again and he never discovered where she was sent or what became of her. Captain Anthony gave him to his daughter, Mrs. Louisa Auld.

Two years later he was sent to Baltimore, Maryland, to work in the household of Louisa Auld's brother-in-law, Hugh Auld, and his wife, Sophia. It was in Baltimore that a curious series of events led to one of the greatest awakenings in Frederick's life.

Sophia began to teach him the alphabet and the rudiments of reading. When her husband discovered her activities he became furious. It was illegal to teach a slave to read. More important, in Hugh's mind, was that an educated slave would no longer want to be a slave. He was afraid, as many other slave owners were, that if slaves were educated, they would all attempt to escape to the Northern states, where slavery was illegal.

Listening to Hugh Auld's infuriated rant, Frederick suddenly understood an important truth that would guide him throughout his life. He learned that education was the path to freedom.

He began to teach himself to read in secret while constantly on guard against discovery. Whenever possible he traded food to poor white children and used them as reading teachers.

He made a giant step forward at the age of 12. After putting together all of the money he earned doing errands, he bought a copy of *The Colombian Orator*. This book helped him to define his speaking style and became an essential part of his life as he taught himself public speaking.

As Auld predicted, Frederick's dissatisfaction with slavery became more evident. Eventually, he was rented out to a "slave breaker" who continually whipped him until he began to feel broken. Somehow he held on and would not let himself be utterly defeated.

He planned his first escape at the age of 18, but the plan was exposed and he was arrested. He expected to be sent to the Deep South, a living death in his mind. However, he was sent back to Hugh Auld in Baltimore.

During his second stay in Baltimore, he even attempted to purchase his own freedom but was unsuccessful. Finally, at the age of 20, he managed to successfully escape. He took a train to Philadelphia, Pennsylvania, avoiding capture by using the borrowed documents of a free black seaman.

In Philadelphia he avoided the slave catchers and quickly moved on to New York City. Feeling safe for the moment, he sent for his fiancée, Anne Murray, a free African-American woman who worked as a maid. They were married on September 15, 1838. Soon thereafter they moved to New Bedford, Massachusetts. It was at this time that Frederick Bailey changed his name to Frederick Douglass in order to avoid recapture.

In New Bedford, Douglass experienced another

life-changing moment. He purchased a copy of an abolitionist newspaper called *The Liberator.* "The paper became my meat and drink," he wrote. "My soul was set all on fire." Douglass became active in every type of antislavery or abolitionist movement he could join.

Two years after his lecture to the people of Cork, Ireland, Frederick Douglass completed his speaking tour. Not only had he convinced many people of the evils of slavery, but his many new friends gathered enough money to purchase his release as a slave. He returned to the United States as a free man.

Upon returning to America, Douglass was able to purchase a printing press and start a newspaper of his own. This newspaper immediately began to compete successfully with the more established abolitionist papers. He worked as hard as he could to influence President Abraham Lincoln to make freedom for slaves one of the major elements of winning the Civil War.

Douglass continued his efforts to help former slaves like himself throughout his life. In later years he was quoted as saying, "Knowledge is the pathway from slavery to freedom."

Frederick Douglass was born into a world without hope. He was torn from his family as a small child. His primary role models early in life were his white masters, people who viewed him as property and treated him like an animal. Yet he never gave up his dreams of freedom and equality for all races and both genders.

He taught himself how to read and how to give speeches while still a slave. He allied himself with as many people and groups as he could who supported his philosophies.

Because of his drive, Frederick Douglass influenced people from all walks of life. He molded himself into a man who made a powerful impact on the highest levels of society in a way that was not thought to be possible.

On February 20, 1895, he died at his home in Washington DC, after returning from a rally of the National Council of Women, where he had received a standing ovation for his efforts in gaining equality for women.

Sir Henry Morton Stanley

British Explorer and Adventurer
(January 28, 1841 – May 10, 1904)

Sir Henry Morton Stanley

"God has furnished us with the necessary senses for the journey of life He has intended we should take. If we employ them wisely, they will take us safely to our journey's end; but if, through their perversion, we misuse them, it will be our own fault. .. We see that the wisdom, moral strength, courage, and patience to guide and sustain us on the way." *(p. 135)*

Taken from The Autobiography of Sir Henry Morton Stanley by Henry Morton Stanley, Lady Dorothy Stanley. Houghton Mifflin Company, The Riverside Press Cambridge, Boston and New York, 1909. Popular Edition published in 1911.

The old English explorer stared out across the waters of Lake Tanganyika in central Africa. As a spasm of pain lanced through his body, his hands tightened around the heavy walking staff. He was tired. Illness etched deep lines around his eyes and his gray beard quivered in the light breeze.

This was Dr. David Livingstone in the year 1870. He was, by all standards, the most famous English explorer in Africa at the time. In the 30 years since he began his career as a missionary in Africa, the so-called "Dark Continent" had thrown her full biological arsenal at him, all the myriad animals, insects, and diseases. Early in his career he was mauled by a lion that left one arm partially paralyzed.

He wanted badly to live long enough to discover the beginnings of the great River Nile. If he accomplished this, his name would live forever.

He felt little fear. He was completely comfortable with his status as the only white man within hundreds of miles in any direction. Unknown to Dr. Livingstone, most of the world assumed him to be dead. Only one of his communications had reached the outside world in six years; all the rest had disappeared before arriving in Zanzibar.

His body was worn out. He was just about finished. He would be dead in little more than two years. Faithful native servants would bury his heart in Africa but return his body to England.

But this is not a story about Dr. Livingstone. It is the chronicle of Henry Morton Stanley, the man sent to find Dr. Livingstone and thereby begin his own legend as one of Africa's greatest explorers.

Sir Henry Morton Stanley was one of those explorers who, through luck, tenacity, skill, and courage, survived where others died. He nearly always achieved success despite overwhelming odds. With each exploration, he pushed the boundaries of knowledge, as well as Western power, into an Africa unexplored by Europeans.

To say that Henry Stanley came from humble beginnings does not begin to tell the tale. Born as John Rowling in a village in northern Wales on January 28, 1841, his christening record labeled him a "bastard" because his parents were unmarried. His father died and his mother gave him to relatives when he was still a baby. The relatives grew tired of the responsibility of raising him and put him in a workhouse when he was six, where he suffered at the hands of older boys and men who saw him as prey.

Released from the workhouse at 15, he went to sea. Shortly after jumping ship in New Orleans, he changed his name to Henry Morton Stanley in honor of a wealthy trader who befriended him and mentored him for the first time in his life.

With the flush of a new name and a new life, Stanley cast off his English roots and declared himself an American. This put him in a difficult position a few years later with the start of the Civil War. Living in the South, he enlisted in the Confederate Army.

Captured by Union forces at the battle of Shiloh, Stanley was given a choice of switching allegiances or suffering in a prison camp. Considering the squalor of the prisoner-of-war camps, he made his decision quickly and was assigned to a Union artillery battery.

The record is unclear about how Stanley left the army. He may have been given a medical discharge because of dysentery. Some think that he may have deserted the Union Army to join the Union Navy. It is known that he served aboard the federal warship *Minnesota* until near the end of the Civil War, when he again jumped ship and returned to Wales.

Seeking to build a reputation as an adventurer, he became a traveling journalist, eventually writing for the *New York Herald*, one of the largest newspapers in the world. His big break came when the managing editor, James Gordon Bennett Jr., sent Stanley to find Dr. Livingstone in Africa.

With virtually unlimited funds from the newspaper, Stanley put together a massive expedition, including over 200 porters. He purchased a magnificent stallion for himself. For security, he organized the safari into five caravans, each leaving at a different time.

He started in January 1870, going first to various other places in Europe and the Middle East on several minor assignments that his editor wanted news of first, before he started into Africa. He eventually began his major African assignment in March 1871. The trip would cover over 700 miles of bush and jungle over a period of 236 days. Nearly everything that could go wrong went wrong.

Within days of departing, Stanley's great stallion died of disease transmitted by a tsetse fly bite. Equipment and native bearers disappeared at an alarming rate. When not able to detour around hostile tribes, his small army of guards was forced to fight their way through. His two European lieutenants died en route. Stanley himself was delirious with fever for much of the trip and constantly considered his death near at hand.

Finally, on November 10, 1871, with only 54 people left in the expedition, he trudged into the village of Ujiji and met Dr. Livingstone with the phrase, "Dr. Livingstone, I presume?" After such a horrific journey, this understated British salutation became a popular catchphrase that is still heard today.

Stanley stayed with Dr. Livingstone for about a month, helping to explore the northern portion of Lake Tanganyika. However, Dr. Livingstone, unwilling to give up his long dream of finding the source of the River Nile, refused to accompany Stanley back to the coast.

Dr. Livingstone failed to discover the origin of the Nile and died on the shores of Lake Baweulu in 1873. When his body was returned to England for burial at Westminster Abbey, Stanley served as a pall-bearer at the funeral.

Stanley's expedition to find Dr. Livingstone made both him and the *New York Herald* famous around the world. He returned to America a hero.

In the coming years, Henry Morton Stanley would make other and much longer journeys into Africa (including one of over 7,000 miles). He was the first European to penetrate so deeply into the heart of Africa. But none of his expeditions proved more famous than his quest to find Dr. Livingstone.

Stanley was always a complex and flamboyant character. He never hesitated to play the part of his own publicist or tout his own accomplishments. This gained him the reputation among some historians as straying from the strict letter of the truth. Others simply regarded him as an inveterate teller of tall tales.

In later years he became the chief explorer for

King Leopold II of Belgium, mapping the Congo River basin. Leopold's rule over the Congo would become so brutal and exploitative that it cast a stain on Stanley as well.

Toward the end of his life, Stanley returned to England. Although his great exploits were a matter of record, and although he was considered a hero in many parts of the world, the British scientific community went out of their way to snub him. This was partially because of his birth and poor beginnings, and partially because he had claimed to be an American for so long.

In the end he was elected to the House of Commons in England and was made a Knight Grand Cross of the Order of Bath. He retired with his wife, Dolly Tennant, to a country estate in Surrey.

He died at the age of 63 on May 10, 1904. His desire to be buried in Westminster Abbey near Dr. Livingstone, however, was denied, perhaps because of the blemished reputation that was a legacy from King Leopold, and perhaps because of the class snobbery that still excluded him from the higher levels of English society.

Louis Armstrong

American Jazz Musician
(August 4, 1901 – July 6, 1971)

Louis Armstrong

"I walked on stage and there I saw something I thought I'd never see. I saw thousands of people, colored and white on the main floor. Not segregated in one row of whites and another row of negroes... These same society people may go around the corner and lynch a Negro. But while they're listening to our music, they don't think about trouble. What's more they're watching Negro and white musicians play side by side. And we bring contentment and pleasure. I always says 'Look at the nice taste we leave. It's bound to mean something. That's what music is for." *(p. 19)*

"You dig what I'm digging?" *(p. 23)*

"I'm a Baptist and a good friend of the Pope's and I always wear a Jewish star a friend gave me for luck." *(p. 34)*

Taken from Louis Armstrong's New Orleans by Thomas Brothers. W. W. Norton and Company. New York 2006.

Whenever anyone talks about the history of jazz musicians, they talk about Louis Armstrong (French pronunciation *Loo-ee*). Without question, he was the greatest cornet and trumpet player of the 20th century, as well as a singer who excelled at "scat" singing which uses wordless syllables. His influence on jazz cannot be overstated.

The greatest era of jazz music stretched from the 1920s to the 1960s, when it was overtaken in popularity by rock 'n' roll and other forms of pop music. Still, it has continued as a beloved art form. Its roots go back as far as the 19th century, with some elements originating from the music of western Africa.

Jazz as a distinct musical form is uniquely American. It began its march to universal recognition in the Deep South, particularly New Orleans. From there it spread northward, especially to Chicago and New York City. It followed the exodus of blacks from the Deep South to the northern cities that offered better pay and an improved lifestyle. It quickly spread to Europe and then throughout the world.

The music itself is hard to define and includes the blues, ragtime, big band swing, and Dixieland. It evolved into Bebop toward the later part of its popularity. It is the music of improvisation, with each performance different from the previous. The music is rarely written down.

It was very common for jazz musicians to give each other nicknames. They called Louis Armstrong "Satchel Mouth" because of his large mouth, which enhanced his intense and strenuous playing style. This name was shortened to "Satchmo" when he toured England and the British people misunderstood the pronunciation of "Satchel Mouth." Armstrong himself appreciated the new name and referred to it in his own book, *Satchmo, My Life in New Orleans.*

The grandson of slaves, Louis Armstrong was born on August 4, 1901, on one of the lowest rungs of the New Orleans social ladder. His father abandoned the family shortly after his birth. His mother left him soon thereafter. His grandmother, Josephine, and his uncle Isaac took over his upbringing.

Mostly unsupervised, he did whatever work a small boy could do, including newspaper delivery and hauling coal. As he made his rounds, it was only natural that he became attracted to the music of the dance halls, brothels, and bars.

He entered the Fisk School for Boys at the age of five but dropped out at eleven. He joined a quartet of other boys and sang on the streets for money. Often in trouble with the law for small things, his life took a dramatic turn when he fired a gun in the air one New Year's Eve. He was sentenced to the New Orleans Home for Colored Waifs.

Captain Joseph Jones, the school administrator, sought to instill discipline and believed that music helped in this regard. He organized a school band and took a special interest in Louis, assigning him the position of band leader. By age 13, Louis began to gain recognition as a first-class cornet player.

Released from the Home at age 14, Louis lived with his father for a while and then with his mother. Most of the time, however, he lived on the streets.

He began to play professionally in bars and dance halls, although he continued to work during the day at whatever job he could find. Eventually, he was given the opportunity to play his music on the Mississippi riverboats.

He called this part of his life the music university.

He learned to read music and matured tremendously as a musician. His style of music also began to solidify.

In his early twenties he left New Orleans for Chicago. There he began to play in Joe "King" Oliver's Creole Jazz Band. The money began flowing in and for the first time in his life, he had a place with his own bathroom. Since he no longer needed to work odd jobs, he concentrated all his energies on his music.

He became known as a virtuoso of the trumpet, a musician without equal or peer. Wherever he went, more experienced trumpet players would challenge his ability to play, sometimes damaging their own lips as they attempted to vanquish Satchmo.

Louis Armstrong played his music throughout his life. He did extensive touring and he recorded whenever possible. He never stopped. He went to Europe, Asia and Australia. He was the ambassador for American jazz around the world, playing for kings and queens.

He survived and prospered as a musician throughout the various changes of jazz, from ragtime to big bands, from solo performances to small groups. He even challenged rock 'n' roll for a time. He never could stop making music—not until there was no more music left in him.

At 63 years of age Louis Armstrong recorded one of his most popular tunes, "Hello, Dolly!" which reached the number one spot on the Billboard Hot 100. Satchmo then was the oldest man to ever record a number-one song. "Hello, Dolly!" knocked the

Beatles from the top of the charts where they had been for 14 straight weeks.

Toward the end of his life, Satchmo gained another nickname as other musicians began to call him Pops, in honor of his elevated status. Louis Armstrong died on July 6, 1971, just four weeks short of his 70th birthday. He was buried at Flushing Cemetery in Queens, New York City.

Those attending his funeral included many of the most famous people in America: politicians, actors, and musicians, including New York Governor Rockefeller, New York City Mayor Lindsay, Duke Ellington, Ella Fitzgerald, Bing Crosby, Frank Sinatra, Johnny Carson, and many others.

William Jefferson (Bill) Clinton

42nd President of the United States
(August 19, 1946 to Present)

William Jefferson (Bill) Clinton

"The point of all that I have said is this: the future is not an inheritance, it is an opportunity and an obligation."

Taken from The Public Papers of the Presidents of the United States, by National Archives and Records Administration, Office of the Federal Registrar, p. 963. Administration of William J. Clinton, 1994/ May 20.

Five United States presidents lost one or more parents while still children. The parents of Andrew Jackson (7th president) died by the time he reached age 14. Herbert Hoover (31st president) was orphaned by the age of nine. The father of Gerald R. Ford (38th president) abandoned his son shortly after birth. Barack Obama (44th president) was born in 1961 and his father left the family in 1964.

The man who would become the 42nd president was born William Jefferson Blythe III, on August 19, 1946, in Hope, Arkansas. His father, a traveling salesman, died in an automobile accident three months before his son's birth.

When Bill was four years old, his mother, Virginia, married Roger Clinton, a man with an automobile dealership in Hot Springs, Arkansas. Bill's stepfather was spoken of as a gambler and an alcoholic who used physical violence against his family. Stories are told about how, when Bill grew big enough, he forcibly stopped his father at times from inflicting more damage on Bill's mother and brother.

Bill attended Hot Springs High School where he excelled as a student leader and musician. He played tenor sax and won first chair in the saxophone section of the state band. For a short time he considered a career in music.

He also considered becoming a doctor. However, when he attended Boys Nation at the age of 16 in 1963, his career locked onto a path from which he would never deviate. As a Boys Nation senator he visited the White House and met President John F. Kennedy. After this, his life changed and public service became his life's dream.

In that same year he experienced a second confirmation of his life's purpose. He heard the Martin Luther King Jr. speech titled "I Have a Dream." The message galvanized him so much that he memorized the entire speech.

In 1968, he received a Bachelor of Science degree in Foreign Service from the Edmund A. Walsh School of Foreign Service at Georgetown University in Washington DC. While there, he joined Alpha Phi Omega, the largest college fraternity in the United States. He was also inducted into Phi Beta Kappa, the nation's oldest honor society. But he considered his summer internship for Arkansas Senator J. William Fulbright as the highlight of his college experience.

He won a Rhodes Scholarship to University

College in Oxford, England, where he studied philosophy, politics, and economics. There he became a fan of rugby, and he tested marijuana, deciding that he loved rugby but not marijuana. Also at Oxford he participated in Vietnam War protests and helped to organize one in October 1969.

He continued his degree work at Yale University Law School, and he received the Juris Doctor degree in 1973. It was at Yale that Clinton met his future wife, Hillary Rodham. They were married on October 11, 1975.

After law school, he accepted a position as a law professor at the University of Arkansas. He ran for Congress in 1974 but lost to the incumbent, Republican John Paul Hammerschmidt. Two years later, in 1976, Clinton was elected the Arkansas Attorney General.

After two years as the Attorney General, Clinton was elected governor of Arkansas at the young age of 32. Two years later, in 1980, he was defeated by Republican Frank T. White. He liked to joke at the time that he was the youngest ex-governor in United States history. (At the time, Arkansas governors were elected for two-year terms.)

Rallying his support, he won the governorship back again in 1982, and he remained the governor for the next ten years. During this time he concentrated on the state's educational system. He also built better roads and transformed Arkansas's economy.

He became an important figure among the "new Democrats," a branch of the Democratic Party that supported smaller government and welfare reform. Then Clinton began to receive national recognition. In 1985, he was chosen to give the Democratic response to President Reagan's State of the Union address.

In 1988, he gave the opening address at the Democratic National Convention. Four years later, Bill Clinton would be selected as the Democratic presidential candidate. But at the time, the road to the presidency seemed a path too narrow and steep for a young governor from Arkansas.

During the Democratic presidential primary campaign of 1992, Clinton barely nudged the needle in the Iowa Caucus, coming in a distant third to Senator Tom Harkin. New Hampshire seemed a sure thing for Massachusetts Senator Paul Tsongas. Yet, after an extraordinary amount of work and an appearance on the television show *60 Minutes* with his wife, Hillary, he very nearly won New Hampshire. The news media crowned him "the comeback kid."

Clinton won big in Florida and Texas. Still, California Governor Jerry Brown remained the frontrunner outside of the Southern states. Clinton set his aim for New York. He won a major victory, discarding his image as a regional candidate.

Finally the Democratic candidate, Bill Clinton was ready to face President George H. W. Bush in the general election. After the first Gulf War, President Bush's approval ratings rose to 80%. Many considered him unbeatable.

But Clinton conducted a masterful campaign.

After storming the country scant weeks before the election with his running mate, Al Gore, Clinton won the election. He won 43% of the vote against George H. W. Bush's 37.4% of the vote. Populist billionaire Ross Perot, an independent, won 18.9% of the vote.

After two terms as President of the United States, Bill Clinton remained active in world politics as an elder statesman. Today Clinton is well recognized for his humanitarian work throughout the world. In many ways he has gained a world-wide constituency.

Aristotle

Greek Philosopher
(384 BC — 322 BC)

Aristotle

"Courage involves pain, and is justly praised; for it is harder to face what is painful than to abstain from what is pleasant."

Taken from the Nicomachean Ethics, III.8 line 39

"Similarly too with courage; for it is by accumstoming ourselves to despise objects of fear and stand up against them that we come to be brave."

Nicomachean Ethics II

A very large head, according to ancient lore, went along with great intellect. Now, however, even cutting-edge science cannot establish whether brain size determines human intelligence. Still, artists like the idea. Cartoons often portray brainy characters with big, ballooning heads.

Ancient history provides one example where a big head cradled a magnificent brain. A Greek bronze statue by Lysippus (330 B.C.) presents Aristotle with an enlarged cranium, worthy of an artist's dreams.

For more than 2,300 years, Western scholars have credited Aristotle with uncommon brilliance, and rightly so. Aristotle studied everything, and everything he studied, he mastered. He wrote on subjects as different from each other as poetry, art, physics, logic, botany, biology, politics, astronomy, music, medicine, and metaphysics (things not provable by human observation), to name only a few.

For centuries the Western world accepted his ideas as fact. His philosophic and scientific conclusions proved so remarkable that few dared to contradict him.

The best minds of the Middle Ages (5th to the 15th century) relied on Aristotle. This is significant because scholars during this time period generally preferred religious texts to guide their world view. Yet, Aristotle considered himself a scientist more than a religious philosopher.

As Europe emerged from the Middle Ages into the Renaissance, the new scientists, poets, and philosophers continued to treat Aristotle as the foundation of wisdom, almost as an intellectual god. Academic debates routinely included quotes from Aristotle as the final authority.

Everyone agrees that the ancient Greek civilization produced some of the best thinkers in human history, not simply for their time in history, but for all time. For people living today, Socrates, Plato, and Aristotle are the three whose names come to mind most quickly when anyone lists the brightest of the ancient Greeks. They are all interconnected.

Socrates, a citizen of Athens born in 469 B.C., was a teacher who developed what is now called the Socratic method, a way of teaching that consisted of asking a succession of hard questions to stimulate critical thinking, in many cases directed at the rich and powerful. The questions forced his students to think more clearly.

Unfortunately for Socrates, this method also established the ignorance of the person being questioned and sometimes created anger and opposition, a dangerous result if the student were a powerful government figure. The aristocracy and politicians of Athens failed to appreciate looking like fools. Eventually, the enemies of Socrates took their opportunity to charge him with corrupting the city's youth. Convicted of this offense, they sentenced him to death by forcing him to drink hemlock, a poison. He died at age 70 in 399 B.C.

His student, Plato, continued his teacher's work and founded the "Academy" in Athens, the Western world's first university. Plato believed that intense mental exercise provided the same benefits for the mind that physical exercise produced on the body. Plato also taught that the world we can know through our senses is only an approximation of the real world, which is perfect and is located in the realm of ideas or outside of matter.

Aristotle was born in 384 B.C. in the northern part of Greece. His father served as a physician to the royal court in Macedonia. Because of his father's position, Aristotle was trained and educated as a member of the aristocracy. When his parents died, Proxenus (his brother-in-law) became his guardian and sent Aristotle to attend Plato's Academy in Athens.

Aristotle spent 20 years studying with Plato and

became his most illustrious student. Regrettably, when Plato died he did not name Aristotle to lead the Academy because Aristotle—even as a student—had begun to disagree with some of Plato's teachings. Aristotle had rejected Plato's version of the "real world" in favor of direct observation of the material world, which has become the basis of all modern science.

Philip, the king of Macedonia, asked Aristotle to come to him and establish the Royal Academy of Macedon—especially to tutor his son Alexander. The historical record leaves little doubt that Aristotle and his student (who would become known as Alexander the Great) became good friends. King Philip died when Alexander was about 18 years old, and immediately the young king set out to conquer the known world. Aristotle returned to Athens where he founded the Lyceum, a university that surpassed Plato's Academy.

Throughout the remainder of his life, Aristotle gathered all the human knowledge available in the world at that time. He studied every subject possible and made contributions to most of them. He succeeded in enlarging the boundaries of knowledge without even the most basic equipment, tools as essential to modern science as clocks and thermometers. But these handicaps did not stop Aristotle from contributing scientific truth to many different fields. Even after 2,300 years, the world today owes a vast debt to Aristotle for his determination to expand his amazing brain and share the results with the world.

Alexander Hamilton

American Founding Father
(January 11, 1755 – July 11, 1804)

Alexander Hamilton

"Real firmness is good for anything; strut is good for nothing."

Taken from Alexander Hamilton: an essay on American union by Frederick Scott Oliver; P. 198. G. P. Putnam's sons, New York, 1921.

In the course of human events, when nations teeter on the edge of chaos, only men and women of extraordinary abilities can tip the scales of history. When they accept the challenge, often at the expense of their own comfort, they imprint their signatures onto the wall of history.

What kind of childhood prepares a great leader to chart the path of history? Logic suggests that a family and society dedicated to the encouragement and support of the child would serve this purpose best. Yet the early life of Alexander Hamilton presents a different pattern.

His family and society failed to protect or prepare him. He suffered destitution and deprivation. His early years were buffeted by the metaphorical winds of desolation. In a strange turn of events, the actual winds of a massive hurricane provided Alexander with his first great opportunity. From there he pulled himself from a rough scrabble existence and defined himself as a man of substance.

Alexander Hamilton earned his place among America's Founding Fathers. He served General George Washington as his chief of staff during the Revolutionary War. He played a significant role in defining the powers and limitations of the Constitution of the United States. As the first Secretary of the Treasury of the United States, he helped to establish a firm financial foundation for the newborn country.

In 1750, Alexander's mother, Rachel, fled an abusive marriage. In her desperation, she abandoned her first son to his father, a German-Jewish merchant planter named Michael Lavien of St. Croix, an island in the British West Indies near Puerto Rico. Escaping to the island of St. Kitts, she fell in love with James A. Hamilton, the fourth son of a Scottish Laird (Lord).

They moved to her birthplace, the island of Nevis, where she gave birth to two children, James Jr., and later Alexander on January 11, 1755. Life was difficult for the unmarried couple. Eventually James Hamilton deserted Rachel and his two boys.

Considered a bastard child by the Church of England, Alexander was not allowed to attend the church school. He educated himself with the help of the 34 books in his family's small library, as well as by taking classes at a private Jewish school.

His mother eked out a living with a small general store but succumbed to a tropical fever and died when Alexander was 13. After her death, Michael Lavien, her original husband whom she had not divorced, stepped forward and seized her tiny estate. When the estate items were auctioned off, a friend purchased the books and returned them to Alexander.

An older cousin agreed to take responsibility for Alexander and his brother James. Unfortunately, almost before they were settled into the household, the cousin, burdened by depression, committed suicide. His death threw their lives into confusion again and the brothers were separated.

James was apprenticed to a carpenter, and Alexander was taken in and adopted by a local merchant, Thomas Stevens. Although devastated by his mother's death, for the first time Alexander was provided with a financially secure home life for the next few years.

On August 30, 1772, an immense hurricane devastated the islands. At the age of 17, Alexander wrote an eye-witness account, published in the *Royal Danish-American Gazette*. The story so impressed the island leadership that leading citizens raised a fund to send Alexander to the American Colonies to complete his education.

In Boston he finished his basic studies and prepared for college. Accepted at King's College (now Columbia University), he moved to New York City in 1774. An advocate for the Revolution, Alexander began to publish articles and essays attacking the Loyalists who supported the King.

He also joined a local militia, the Hearts of Oak.

At their first battle in 1775, he led them to capture the British cannon at the New York Battery. With captured weapons, he formed an artillery company and was elected its captain.

In 1776, at the Battle of Trenton, his artillery kept the Hessians (German regiments hired by the British) pinned near the Trenton Barracks and helped to win the battle. A year later, General George Washington invited Hamilton to join his staff as his personal aide with a rank of lieutenant colonel.

Near the end of the war, Hamilton pleaded with Washington to allow him to return to a fighting battalion. General Washington gave him three battalions of New York light infantry. In the battle of Yorktown they stormed and captured a major British fortification.

The success of the Revolutionary War stunned the world. The fact that a confederation of 13 colonies managed to defeat the British, considered the best army in the world, shattered historic precedent.

But winning the war did not establish America as a nation. Ending the war was merely the beginning of the process. Crafting the world's first written Constitution launched the great American Experiment and changed the world forever.

Hamilton became deeply committed to creating the Constitution. Not all of his ideas became a part of the final document. He put forth the idea, for example, that the President and Senators should hold office for life. He also wanted state governors appointed by the federal government rather than elected by the people. Today, few Americans would agree with Hamilton on these issues.

However, Hamilton acted as a practical politician. He supported and signed the final draft of the Constitution. Further, he devoted great effort to assure that it was ratified by initiating what would be known as *The Federalist Papers*, one of his greatest legacies. To do so, Hamilton joined forces with John Jay (future Chief Justice of the Supreme Court) and James Madison (4th President of the United States). Each man wrote a series of essays, printed in newspapers and other public forums, explaining why the Constitution should be ratified. Hamilton wrote two thirds of the 85 total essays; Madison wrote most of the rest and Jay wrote five. Their efforts won the popular acceptance of the Constitution. Even today, *The Federalist Papers* are a primary source for interpreting the Constitution.

As the Treasury Secretary under President George Washington, Hamilton struggled to put the nation on a firm financial footing. He established the first mint and the nation's first national bank. He helped pass legislation to nationalize the huge debt created by the Revolutionary War. He also established a coastal navy to catch smugglers, which was eventually expanded and became the United States Coast Guard.

Hamilton also enjoyed behind-the-scenes manipulation of politics. Although Thomas Jefferson and Hamilton were opposites in nearly everything political, Hamilton felt a much greater antagonism for Aaron Burr, another New York politician. In the presidential election of 1800, Hamilton acted to ensure that Jefferson became president over Burr. This increased the long and bitter personal and political antagonism between the two men.

Again, in 1804 when Aaron Burr wanted to become the governor of New York, Hamilton worked to stop him. Finally, Burr accused Hamilton of a personal slur and challenged him to a duel, which became the most infamous duel in American history.

Since dueling was illegal in New York and considered a type of murder, the two men traveled to New Jersey on July 11, 1804. Hamilton's shot went high, but Burr's bullet penetrated Alexander's liver and lodged in his spine. Alexander Hamilton died the following afternoon, July 12, 1804.

Steve Jobs

American Inventor and Businessman
Founder of Apple, Inc.
(February 24, 1955 – October 5, 2011)

Steve Jobs

"For the past 33 years, I have looked in the mirror every morning and asked myself: 'If today were the last day of my life, would I want to do what I am about to do today?' And whenever the answer has been 'No' for too many days in a row, I know I need to change something."

Taken from Identity – Your Passport to Success by Stedman Graham, p. 91 (chapter written by Steve Jobs). Pearson Education, Inc. Publishing as FT press. Upper Saddle River, New Jersey, 2012.

"Sometimes life hits you in the head with a brick. Don't lose faith." *(Graham, 2012. P. 91)*

"Don't let the noise of others' opinions drown out your own inner voice...have the courage to follow your heart and intuition." *(Graham, 2012. P 94)*

What does a young man do after he starts a business in his garage, becomes a millionaire and famous, is called a genius, gets thrown out of his own business, gets mad and then becomes a billionaire? For an encore he develops three of the hottest tech devices in the world!

Born in San Francisco, Steve was adopted at birth by Paul and Clara Jobs. Although much later in life he searched for and discovered the identities of his birth parents, he considered Paul and Clara his true parents "1000 percent."

The elder Jobs was a machinist by trade and always a genius with his hands, according to Steve. He remembered his father setting aside a portion of the home workbench and teaching him how to take things apart and reassemble them.

While attending Homestead High School in Cupertino, Steve was hired by Hewlett-Packard as a summer employee. There he met Steve Wozniak, his future partner in the founding of Apple Computer, Inc.

After graduating in 1972, Steve attended Reed College in Portland, Oregon, but he dropped out after only one semester. He continued to audit classes and credits his attendance at a calligraphy class for his enthusiasm for proportional fonts and various typefaces on the Macintosh (Mac) computer.

He returned to California in 1974, where he became involved in the Homebrew Computer Club, the brainchild of Steve Wozniak. He also took a job with Atari, one of the early video game manufacturers, but only long enough to save money for a trip to India.

In India he sought spiritual and philosophical enlightenment. He again returned to California, this time with his head shaved and wearing the traditional garments of India. His time as a seeker of enlightenment in India proved a watershed for Jobs. He later said that those who did not understand and share his countercultural roots could not understand many aspects of his thinking.

On his return to Atari, he joined with Steve Wozniak on a project to create a new circuit board for the game *Breakout*. Atari promised to pay them $100 for each computer chip that they could eliminate from the board. They eliminated over 50 chips. But the design was so sophisticated that it was impossible to reproduce on the assembly line. Atari paid them only $700 instead of the $5,000 they felt they were owed.

During this period Wozniak began designing a new type of computer, one simple and inexpensive enough for an individual but as powerful as the available micro-processing chips would allow. Jobs was intrigued by the design. He believed that the machine held tremendous commercial potential and convinced Wozniak that they should begin assembling the computer and selling it.

They began their manufacturing adventure in whatever space they could find, including friends' homes and garages. They financed the venture by selling whatever they owned, including a VW bus and their calculators. By scrounging money and using whatever space was available, they produced 200 copies of the computer they named the Apple I.

Their small company grew and flourished. It quickly became obvious that they needed help from people more experienced in the business world. In 1983, Jobs convinced John Sculley, then president of Pepsi-Cola, to leave his job and to become the head of Apple Computer as the chief executive officer.

In 1984, Apple released one of the most famous television commercials of all time. It first played during Super Bowl XVIII and announced the release of the Macintosh computer. It featured a young woman bursting into an auditorium full of human drones watching a massive computer screen. She swung a large hammer and released it, shattering the wall-sized computer screen. The message was clear: the Macintosh would release the computer masses from cyber slavery.

There is no secret that Jobs was a temperamental manager—highly emotional at moments and hard as steel at others. He functioned within what many would come to call a "reality distortion field." Exceptionally persuasive, he expected and received extraordinary results, often at the expense of others.

Within a year after the release of Macintosh, a political battle developed within the hierarchy of the company itself. The two main players were the radical computer genius, Steve Jobs, and the powerful businessman and CEO, John Sculley. Sculley won the battle and relieved Jobs of all his duties within the company. Disgusted, Jobs left.

For a short time Steve pondered how his world had changed almost overnight. He wondered how his dream could be taken away from him. He wasted very little time, however, developing and founding NeXT Computer in 1985, targeted to the financial, scientific, and academic community. The machine he produced was technologically brilliant, near aesthetically perfect, but too expensive. The company's first profitable year was 1994.

In 1986, he purchased a little company called The Graphics Group for $10 million, which would later be renamed Pixar. *Toy Story* was their first full-length film. It became a massive success, followed by others, including *Finding Nemo, Cars, WALL-E,* and *Ratatouille,* to name a few. In 2006, Disney agreed to purchase Pixar for $7.4 billion. This made Steve Jobs the largest single shareholder of the Walt Disney Company stock.

In 1996, Apple purchased Steve's company NeXT Computer for $429 million, bringing Jobs back into Apple. He became the temporary chief executive in 1998. He named himself as permanent CEO in 2000. Under the guidance of Steve Jobs, who had gained a great deal of wisdom and knowledge since the early days of building computers in his garage, Apple became one of the most profitable and innovative tech companies in the world.

In 2001, the company introduced the iPod. It was not the first portable media player. Still, it swept the market, becoming the standard. The 2007 introduction of the iPhone set the cellular world on its ear, again setting the standard all cellular phones must follow.

Apple launched the iPad in 2010. For more than a decade the computer industry dreamed of a workable "tablet computer." Apple made its first attempt in 1993 with the Newton. Then, with the introduction of the iPad, Apple set the standard for a third time.

The rest of the industry scrambled to catch up with the leader.

Steve Jobs was diagnosed with pancreatic cancer in 2003. For years, he kept his disease from the public. In his keynote address at Apple's 2006 conference he looked very thin, almost emaciated. An Apple spokesman released a statement that "Steve's health is robust." Although he continued to wage a furious battle against the disease, he died at home on October 5, 2011.

Johann Sebastian Bach

German Music Composer
(March 31, 1685 – July 28, 1750)

Johann Sebastian Bach

"I was made to work; if you are equally industrious you will be equally successful."

Taken from Johann Sebastian Bach: his life, art, and Work translated from the German by Johann Nikolaus Forkel, p. 106. New York, Harcourt, Brace, and Howe, 1920.

Nearly everyone has heard the name Johann Sebastian Bach, one of the world's greatest musicians. Today, over 325 years since his birth, the popularity of his toccatas, fugues, cantatas, canons, and choral preludes is greater than at any time during his life.

Yet, to fully understand the sublime music of Bach is almost like learning a foreign language. The very style and nature of his music poses a challenge for modern, young music enthusiasts who are more attuned to rap, rhythm & blues, hip hop, country, and rock 'n' roll.

Today, those who truly love Bach do not hesitate to immerse themselves in ever more complex and tortuous classes on music performance, history, and appreciation. On the other hand, simply listening to his music with an open mind can provide many hours of enjoyment and the essence of understanding his musical brilliance.

Johann Sebastian Bach was born in Germany during the latter part of the 17th century in 1685, to a family overflowing with musical talent. His father, all of his uncles, and his older siblings were musicians, ranging from church organists to court chamber musicians to composers. Many of Bach's children also became accomplished musicians in their own right.

He was orphaned before he reached the age of ten, when his mother and then his father died eight months apart. Stunned and staggered by their deaths, Johann went to live with his eldest brother, who played the organ at a nearby church.

Johann Sebastian Bach went to a choral school for two years when he was 14, and after he graduated, he sought one or another musical post with wealthy patrons. For a short period of time, he repaired and maintained organs and other musical instruments. He was a very talented technician. He also began composing his own music. Later in life he continued to personally maintain his large collection of musical instruments.

His professional career flourished, even as a young man. By the standards of the time, any skilled or even extraordinary musicians would count themselves lucky to succeed so quickly. Still, Bach wanted more—more recognition, more freedom to compose what he wanted, greater financial rewards.

At 18 he became the court musician in the chapel of Duke Johann Ernst in Weimar. By age 21, he was offered a more financially lucrative position as an organist and later choirmaster at St. Blasius. Then he returned to the Duke Ernst's court in Weimar where he received a magnificent salary and a luxurious apartment within a five-minute walk from the ducal palace, until he fell out of favor.

Falling out of favor became a pattern for Bach's professional life. His genius impressed the most aristocratic patrons. Still, his demands for better working conditions and his attitude of self-importance infuriated his employers. His ability to irritate his employers almost rivaled his contempt for the people whose money provided him with food and shelter. He belittled his patrons because they knew so little about music. They did not appreciate the complexities of music that were so important to him.

At one point during his second employment at Weimar he was jailed for 30 days. Upon release he was dismissed from his position as concertmaster and organist. Still the next wealthy patron did not hesitate to step forward. Prince Leopold offered him a position as his director of music.

Bach married twice in his life. His first wife gave him seven children, and after she died, Bach married again and had thirteen more children. With such a large family, finances were always tight. Despite his prestigious career, he constantly sought for new ways to make money.

Motivated by the burden to support such a family, he readily accepted commissions to compose new pieces of music for weddings, funerals, and all other occasions. This required him to write extremely complicated pieces of music with only a few days' notice. He sold music books. He bought and sold instruments. But composing music on demand proved to be his primary method of providing for the family.

During his lifetime Bach failed to receive the professional recognition he deserved. Of his nearly 1,000 musical compositions that survive today, only a dozen were widely published during his life. Some were printed at his own expense. For example, today there are more than 70 recordings of his famous Brandenburg Concertos available commercially. None of these were published until 1850, 100 years after Bach's death.

Above all else, Bach was a spiritual man. He lived and composed music at a time when almost all aspects of life were interwoven with the German Lutheran Church. Virtually all of his music contained a religious theme. He excelled in this format, inspiring and uplifting even those who claimed to have no faith at all.

Art Linkletter

Radio and Television Personality

(July 17, 1912 - May 26, 2010)

Art Linkletter

"For many, scientific studies are a moot point. If you believe that the power of Jesus can heal the sick, you're going to believe it even if one hundred Stanford Laboratory studies say otherwise. Such is the resilience of faith." *(p. 195)*

"Physicists and experts in relativity will tell you that there is no such thing as time travel. Nonsense. Time travel is real; it exists in our minds. We choose to live forward or backward, in the future or the past, all while our bodies continue to exist in the present.

"Regret, or the lack of it, is the only real time machine. Regret is the fuel behind the dark negative clouds that some older people seem to live under...

"One more thing about regret: it's a mistake reminding you to learn. Don't relive your regrets but learn from them." *(214-215)*

Taken from How to make the Rest of Your Life the Best of Your Life by Mark Victor Hansen and Art Linkletter. Nashville, Tennessee by Thomas Nelson, Inc. 2006.

Some people have all the luck. The ultra-successful live a charmed life—or so it seems. One fine day *success* simply drove down their street, turned up into their driveway and parked in their garage. Fully satisfied, it never left.

Art Linkletter, entertainer extraordinaire for much of the 20th century, appeared to own the recipe for success, stepping from triumph to triumph without hesitation. Everyone who watched television during the 1950s, '60s and '70s knew the name and face of Art Linkletter.

Americans welcomed him into their living rooms like a favorite uncle overloaded with presents. He possessed the ability to embrace his audience from afar, as if they were individuals, as if he were sitting across the kitchen table. No one could doubt the passion for his work; he radiated enthusiasm and good cheer.

But like almost every person who has reached the pinnacle of their profession, the long list of accomplishments does not tell the entire tale.

He credited his many achievements to his lifelong determination to move forward despite the circumstances and his willingness to take risks. At the age of 94 he made the point that his successes were rooted in his ability to shrug off adversity and keep going.

Art Linkletter, whose birth name was Gordon Arthur Kelly, was born in Moose Jaw, Saskatchewan, Canada on July 17, 1912. Abandoned at birth, Art was adopted by John and Mary Linkletter as a baby. His adoptive father worked as a preacher on Sundays. Unable to make ends meet as a small-town pastor, he worked as a shoemaker during the rest of the week.

The family remained poor throughout Art's childhood. Art even lived the life of a hobo for a short time, hopping freight trains to move from town to town, before deciding to enter college in San Diego, California.

Art began his entertainment career during the Great Depression of the 1930s while still attending college in San Diego. He was a radio and sports announcer. From there he went to a bigger market in Dallas, Texas and then to San Francisco.

He became a popular radio host for the ABC and CBS networks in the 1940s and early 1950s. Six of his shows were syndicated nationally and many of the most famous entertainers of the time appeared on his radio programs, including Groucho Marx and a very young Johnny Carson, the legendary *Tonight Show* host before Jay Leno.

In the 1950s he moved to television. During this time there were only three network channels, CBS, NBC, and ABC. He was the only person ever to participate on a television program on all three networks at the same time. At one point he hosted five shows running at different time periods.

He hosted a show called *House Party* five days a week on CBS. *Life with Linkletter* aired on ABC during the middle of the week, and *People Are Funny* was a Friday night standard on NBC. *People Are Funny* ran for 19 consecutive years and *House Party* for 26 years, two of the longest-running shows in the history of television.

During his life Art Linkletter wrote 28 books. Many made the bestseller lists, some for more than a year. He released his final book at age 94, *How to Make the Rest of Your Life the Best of Your Life*.

Without question Linkletter gained the most fame for his live interviews with children between the ages of five and ten. He always took whatever a child told him seriously. Some of his interviews, recorded in his book *Kids Say the Darndest Things,* are extremely funny.

Linkletter almost took a different path early in his entertainment career. He worked as a local radio announcer, receiving only $70 a month. As a sports announcer he received just $15 for each football game. He had reached the decision to quit the radio business and become a teacher when he heard about a fellow in Texas who had tried something entirely new.

Stretching a long microphone cord out the studio window, the Texas man conducted street interviews. Young Linkletter understood the potential immediately. From that time forward he decided to base his career on talking to people.

A few years later his career hit a wall. Working his dream job as the radio director for the San Francisco World's Fair, he was fired. The president of the fair wanted a more dramatic opening and suggested an impossible stunt. When Linkletter responded with the words, "You're nuts," he was told to pack his things and leave the office.

Rather than fall apart under the devastating blow, Linkletter decided to move ahead in a different direction. For him this was the trigger. From that point forward he never again allowed himself to stray into an employer-employee relationship. He functioned as his own agent, promoted his own sales, produced his own shows, and never allowed another manager to tell him what to do.

Art Linkletter died on May 26, 2010, at his home, at the age of 97. Yet, he left a legacy of achievement. He never hesitated to take a chance. He did not fear to start small, trusting that his abilities would result in success, and he was right.

Eleanor Roosevelt

U.S. First Lady (1933-1945)
Speaker, Author, Civil Rights Activist
(October 11, 1884 – November 7, 1962)

Eleanor Roosevelt

"I had a great curiosity about life and a desire to participate in every experience that might be the lot of a woman." *(p.41)*

Taken from The Autobiography of Eleanor Roosevelt by Eleanor Roosevelt. Harper & Brothers, New York, 1961.

"You gain strength, courage and confidence by every experience in which you really stop to look fear in the face... you must do the thing you think you cannot do."

Taken from Eleanor Roosevelt – A Life of Discovery by Russell Freedman. Clarion Books a Houghton Mifflin Company. New York, 1993, pi.

The children's story "The Ugly Duckling" by Hans Christian Andersen tells the tale of a strikingly homely little duck. The other barnyard animals derived endless hours of delight in pointing out the unattractive truth, at least for a time. Eventually the ugly duckling matured and transformed into a swan, the most regal and elegant of all water birds.

Eleanor Anna Roosevelt thought of herself as an ugly duckling. Her mirror told her the truth. Others did not hesitate to confirm her suspicions. She did not meet the minimum standards of beauty and grace for her gender and—more important—of her high social and economic class.

As the years progressed, Eleanor failed to evolve

into anything she or others could look upon with visual satisfaction. She never became the swan. Her inelegant and angular features simply matured.

Instead, she developed into a woman of great substance, moral character, and unyielding quality. America has produced few women of her greatness and distinction.

For 12 of her 78 years, Eleanor Roosevelt was the First Lady of the United States, the wife of President Franklin Delano Roosevelt. She accomplished much during those years in the White House, but her energy and determination to do good did not begin with her husband's political success nor end with her husband's death. Eleanor Roosevelt knew for herself the price of character. From an early age she prepared herself for great challenges. History records the choices she made that led to her success.

Anna Eleanor Roosevelt was born in late 1884 to a family of wealth and privilege. But her young years found little of the nurturing that brings a child to smile easily and often. Her mother counted her as a future failure because Eleanor was unattractive and solemn in her manner from the start.

Eleanor's father loved his "little Nell," but even as a young man Elliot Roosevelt was an alcoholic. Their happy moments together were too few. When Eleanor was six, her Uncle Teddy—the future president Theodore Roosevelt—sent her father to a sanitarium in France to be cured of alcoholism. When Eleanor was eight, her mother died of diphtheria. Two years later her father died far from home, with only his alcohol for company instead of his family. By her own account, Eleanor never smiled during this period.

Eleanor's Grandma Hall took responsibility for Eleanor and her two brothers. Eleanor found herself in a somewhat better environment for a growing young woman, though not by much. She rarely felt useful or loved or needed or appreciated. Still, something within her grew. Early in her teenage years she discovered that notwithstanding the plainness of a woman's face, all people would be attracted if they perceived truth and loyalty in the features. In this, young Eleanor chose to grow into the strength of character that made all the future choices of her life possible.

When she was 15, her family decided to send her to a finishing school in England. There she was but one among many wealthy and beautiful young women. Yet, the headmistress saw great potential in Eleanor and reached out to the young American girl. Madame Souvestre not only taught Eleanor about the protocols and manners of upper class society, she shared bold ideas about how a woman could be a force for good in the world. Eleanor responded to these ideas and ideals. She carried them into her life with the strength of her own conviction.

Eleanor returned to the States at 18. She volunteered as a social worker in the poorest parts of New York City. She met her father's fifth cousin and future husband, Franklin D. Roosevelt. Franklin was a handsome man that many young women hoped to marry. Later, when asked why he chose Eleanor, Franklin said that Eleanor's willingness to work among the poor impressed him very much. They married in 1905.

Although Roosevelt men were well positioned to choose a life of politics, less was expected of the Roosevelt women. Eleanor could have chosen a worry-free life enjoying her family's wealth. Instead, she taught at a local school and wrote articles for newspapers and magazines. She continued her volunteer social work in slums, hospitals, asylums and prisons.

When Franklin won a seat as a New York State Senator in 1910, they moved to Albany, New York, and Eleanor found her interest in politics growing. In 1915, President Wilson appointed Franklin as Under Secretary of the Navy. They moved to Washington DC.

In 1921, Franklin suffered an infection, possibly polio, which left his legs paralyzed. Eleanor nursed him through the difficult first weeks and months. She began to attend meetings in his place, especially when the location was difficult to reach with a wheelchair. In time, Franklin spoke of her as his eyes, ears, and feet. The experience she gained, mingled with her own sense of moral balance and her own vision of what could be, gave confidence to her voice.

After Franklin had gained enough strength to return to public life, he leaned on Eleanor more than ever. Their strength as a team proved to be equal to more and more demanding opportunities, until finally they found themselves in Washington as President and First Lady.

Eleanor knew that little was expected of First Ladies. For Eleanor, that would not do. Before her marriage she learned firsthand of the needs of the poor. Then, as a politician's wife for many years, she had time to think about America's potential and how the government could do its part in realizing that potential. In the White House she pursued these goals, which required her to do a tremendous amount of work in addition to her social duties as the First Lady.

As First Lady, she kept a rigorous and productive schedule. Women throughout America followed her daily newspaper column, "My Day." They delighted to see a strong woman making her own success in so many ways.

When America entered World War II, she was prepared to contribute as never before. She arranged to tour military hospitals around the world. She co-chaired the National Committee on Civil Defense. She volunteered to tour Latin America on a good-will tour.

When Franklin died in 1945, Eleanor could have stepped off the national and world stages. She chose to remain active in politics for many more years. She found her voice. There was still much good to do.

President Truman appointed Eleanor Roosevelt as a delegate to the newly formed United Nations.

She co-authored the UN Universal Declaration of Human Rights. Her lifetime had prepared her for that work as perhaps no other figure in the world. She personally visited, comforted, and lifted thousands who were suffering.

By the time she died on November 7, 1962, Eleanor Roosevelt had accomplished much during her life. Much had depended on her ability to break with tradition, a known and safe path, and to choose her own way. America was a nation fortunate to call her its daughter.

Babe Ruth

American Baseball Player
(February 6, 1895 – August 16, 1948)

Babe Ruth

"The people who cheer me from the stands or write me letters aren't interested so much in Babe Ruth as they are in something else. They're interested in baseball.

"All players realize that sooner or later.

"What a game it is!" *(p. 16)*

"If you happen to be a baseball fan who reads the newspapers you've probably noticed that before a world series or any other big series the writers always print long stories of comparisons between individual players... That's interesting – but as far as doping out the winner of the series is concerned, it's bunk... For ball players know that it isn't individuals who count. It's the way a team plays as a whole, that determines its offensive power or its defensive strength." *(p. 19-20)*

"Pitchers, real pitchers – learn early that their job isn't so much to keep opposing batsmen from hitting as it is to make them hit at someone. The trouble with most kid pitchers is that they forget there are eight other men on the team to help them." *(p. 32)*

Taken from Babe Ruth's Own Book of Baseball by George Herman Ruth. G. P. Putnam's Sons, New York, 1928.

George Herman Ruth Jr. lived life large. Yet, because of his background and upbringing, he lacked refinement and the social skills most people expected from an international role model. At times he was a bit coarse, some would say crude. Still, people were drawn to his engaging demeanor and lively personality.

On the playing field Babe Ruth made himself into one of the most famous baseball players of all time and one of the greatest athletes to play any sport. Off the playing field, his large appetites for the nightclub life, food, women, and alcohol were notorious. People described him as a partier, a jokester, and a prankster. He considered the entire world his playground.

Today, many scientists believe that Babe Ruth suffered from ADHD (attention deficit hyperactivity disorder). It is a condition characterized by becoming easily bored, having a hard time staying focused and being always on the go. Still, while ADHD may have contributed to his bigger-than-life behavior in his private life, it may have helped his baseball career. ADHD is also known to enhance a particular ability when the mind is completely engaged. Other famous people with ADHD include Albert Einstein, Winston Churchill, and Thomas Edison.

His adopted daughter, Julia Ruth Stevens, offered a different viewpoint on his love of life and out-of-bounds lifestyle. She recalled his difficult childhood and suggested that because of the deprivations, he felt driven to fill up with everything available to make up for the times of unfulfilled need.

Indeed, Babe experienced a childhood that few would envy. Born on February 6, 1895, in Baltimore, Maryland, his father, George Herman Ruth Sr., tended bar and eventually owned his own tavern. His mother, Kate Schamberger-Ruth, labored alongside her husband and together they worked long hours.

Unmonitored by his parents, by age seven George was considered an incorrigible kid, running free among the docks of the central harbor and the terminals of the Baltimore and Ohio Railroad. Constantly in trouble, he threw tomatoes at police officers and began mimicking the behavior of dockyard workers. Even at such a young age he began chewing tobacco and drinking alcohol.

Unable to cope with or control their child, his parents determined that George needed a more disciplined environment. His father signed over guardianship to the Catholic monks of St. Mary's Industrial School. This was an entirely different world, part trade school, part orphanage, and part reform school.

St. Mary's housed up to 300 youths in a barracks environment, surrounded by high walls. The monks strictly enforced discipline. George lived there for the next 12 years, rarely seeing his parents because they seldom visited him.

At St. Mary's he became acquainted with the two greatest influences of his young life, baseball and Brother Matthias, the prefect of discipline at the school. Brother Matthias took a special interest in George. Although Brother Matthias was a stern person and strict disciplinarian, he was also kind. As George grew older, Brother Matthias taught him to play baseball.

By age 19, George had become one of the stars in the multiple baseball leagues organized within the walls of St. Mary's. In 1914, Jack Dunn, the owner of the minor league team the Baltimore Orioles, learned of George's prowess and signed him as a pitcher. Still considered a minor, Jack became his legal guardian in order to sign him to a professional team.

When the other players saw the young man following closely after Jack, one of them is said to have called out, "Look at Dunn and his new babe." The nickname stuck and George became known as Babe Ruth. Other nicknames that he gathered during its great career were "the Bambino" and the "Sultan of Swat."

After the confines, the discipline, and the regimentation of St. Mary's School, Ruth blossomed in his newfound freedom and quickly proved his ability as a baseball player. Although signed at $100 per month, by May his salary doubled. It increased again the following month. Before the end of his first season, in July 1914, he was sold to a major league team, the Boston Red Sox, which paid him a salary of $3,500 a season. Still a first-year rookie, he met a 17-year-old waitress named Helen Woodford and married her in October 1914.

Ruth became a star during his three seasons with the Boston Red Sox, helping them to win two World Series. But things changed when new ownership took over the ball club. In December 1919, the new owner, Harry Frazee, wanted to produce a Broadway play.

He sold Babe Ruth to the New York Yankees for $100,000, the largest amount ever paid at that time for a major league ballplayer.

Despite the large sum, baseball historians consider this trade the worst in the history of professional sports. Not only did Mr. Frazee's play flop, but the Yankees, a team that had never won a pennant before, went on to win 39 American League pennants and 26 World Series. The Red Sox suffered from what became known as the "Curse of the Bambino." They did not win another World Series until 2004.

While playing for the Yankees, Babe Ruth invigorated not only the team but the entire sport. The popularity of baseball exploded in the 1920s, in large part because of Ruth's abilities and enthusiasm. During his career he sustained an overall batting average of .342. He was the first player to hit 60 home runs in one season, a record that stood for 34 years until broken in 1961 by Roger Maris. His lifetime record of 714 home runs was a record for 39 years, finally broken by Hank Aaron in 1974.

Ruth loved the crowds and loved the limelight of New York City. He could never get enough attention from his fans. But his wife, Helen, did not enjoy Ruth's celebrity and lifestyle. They adopted a baby girl in 1921 and named her Dorothy, but this was not enough to keep them together. They continued to drift apart and Helen finally moved back to Sudbury, Massachusetts, with Dorothy. Although Babe and Helen lived apart, because they were Catholics they did not divorce.

In 1923, Ruth met Claire Hodgson, a native of Athens, Georgia. Claire had moved to New York to pursue a career in show business. She found success as a model and showgirl. Ruth thought her to be intelligent, energetic, and self assured.

In January 1929, Ruth's wife, Helen, died in a tragic house fire. In April that year he married Claire and she became the love of his life. He finally had the big family he wanted, which included not only his daughter, Dorothy, but also Claire's daughter, Julia, Claire's two brothers and her mother.

Throughout his career as a ballplayer and afterward Babe Ruth demonstrated an unwavering kindness for children. He never refused to sign an autograph for a child. In the 1930s, after St. Mary's Industrial School suffered a major fire, he organized a fundraising drive that raised over $100,000.

In the fall of 1946, Babe Ruth was found to have cancer in his neck. He died on August 16, 1948, at the age of 53. His body lay in state for two days at the entrance of Yankee Stadium. More than 100,000 people came to pay their final respects.

William Tecumseh Sherman

U.S. General – American Civil War
(February 8, 1820 – February 14, 1891)

William Tecumseh Sherman

"Be steadfast, therefore my countrymen! Be not too easily or too hastily alarmed; but bear in mind that vigilance is the price of liberty, and courage the prime essential of justice." *(p. 11)*

"I now hope and beg, that all good men South and North will unite in real earnest to repair the mistakes and wrong of the past." *(P. 9)*

Taken from General William T. Sherman's address: (New York City, May 30th. 1878, p. 11, Harvard College Library, 1878 – privately printed)

"War is hell." *(p.310)*

"The bluer the times the more closely should one cling to his country." *(p. 93)*

Taken from Sherman: soldier, realist, American by B.H. Liddell Hart. Originally published: Boston: Dodd, Mead & Co., 1929.

Towards the end of the American Civil War, the armies of Union General William Tecumseh Sherman cut a wide swath of destruction on his "March to the Sea." He called his scorched earth campaign the "hard war"—burning Atlanta, attacking Savannah, and ravaging much of South and North Carolina.

He laid waste to the South's ability to supply and feed their armies. In effect, the calculated destruction of both military and civilian property broke the back of the Confederate war effort.

Later he would write about this strategy of total warfare, saying, "My aim then was to whip the rebels, to humble their pride, to follow them to their innermost recesses. . . ." Nearly 150 years later, for many Southerners he is still the most despised man in the history of the South.

Photographs and portraits of General Sherman display an unapologetic man, staring into the distance with disapproval. He possessed a face full of creases and hard edges, with predatory eyes as piercing and deadly as any great hunting bird.

William Tecumseh Sherman was one of history's great warriors. This is not to name him a noble man, nor to accuse him of malice. All great warriors are loved by some and hated with unwavering bitterness by others.

Born on February 8, 1820, in Lancaster, Ohio, William suffered the death of his father in 1829, which left the family without financial support. His mother, desperate and unable to care for 11 children, sent nine-year-old William to live with neighbors, the Thomas Ewing family.

When William was 16, his foster father, then a United States senator, secured an appointment for him to the United States Military Academy at West Point. William excelled academically but never demonstrated any fondness for the rules of military life, nor for the strict neatness of military dress. As a result he was never promoted and remained a private throughout his four years at the Academy.

Commissioned a second lieutenant of artillery upon graduation, Sherman participated in the second Seminole War in Florida. Later, assigned to the newly acquired territory of California, he was discouraged by missing the promotion opportunities available in the Mexican-American War, which lasted from 1846 to 1848. He resigned his commission after being promoted to captain in 1850.

Sherman met with one disaster after another as a civilian. The bank he managed in San Francisco went bust. He was transferred to a bank in New York, but that one failed as well. He then tried his hand as a lawyer in Leavenworth, Kansas, but without much success.

Finally, in 1859, Sherman received an appointment as the superintendent at the Louisiana State Seminary of Learning and Military Academy, which would later become Louisiana State University. In this position he flourished. People said he was created for the job.

Unfortunately, within two years the Southern states began to talk about secession from the Union. Sherman left Louisiana telling his Southern friends, "You people of the South don't know what you're doing. This country will be drenched in blood, and God only knows how it will end. It is all folly, madness, a crime against civilization!"

Returning to Washington DC, he was appalled by the lack of preparation for war. Eventually he received a commission as a colonel of the 13th United States Infantry Regiment. He participated in the first Battle of Bull Run. Although the battle proved disastrous for the Union Army, Sherman distinguished himself. Abraham Lincoln promoted him to the rank of brigadier general of volunteers.

Transferred to the Western theater of the war, Sherman suffered from melancholy and deep depression. At times even the newspapers baldly labeled him as insane, which was untrue. He asked to be relieved of command.

After his return to duty some months later, he was placed under the command of General Ulysses S. Grant. This was a duty he relished. On the first day of the Battle of Shiloh on April 6, 1862, the Confederate forces pushed the Union forces into a retreat. Sherman rallied his troops, stopping a complete collapse. The next day Sherman helped to lead a Union counterattack, being wounded twice and having three horses shot out from under him. For this he was promoted to major general of volunteers.

William T. Sherman became the commanding general of the Western theater of the war when President Lincoln called General Grant to defend Washington as the commanding general. In 1864, Sherman developed a plan to cut the South in half and destroy its ability to provide food and other supplies to its armed forces. He entered Georgia with three armies totaling about 100,000 men and fought his way to Atlanta.

Both Grant and Lincoln encouraged Sherman to destroy as much property as possible and thereby weaken the Southern war effort. His capture of Atlanta also provided the momentum that Lincoln needed to secure his second term as president in 1864.

After Atlanta, Sherman turned his army toward Savannah, Georgia. From there he marched into South Carolina. Sherman wanted to punish South Carolina for being the first state to secede from the Union. The destruction proved much worse than anything in Georgia.

He marched his army into North Carolina. There, shortly after General Robert E. Lee's April 9, 1865 surrender to General Ulysses S. Grant at Appomattox Courthouse and Abraham Lincoln's assassination five days later, General Sherman accepted the surrender of his opponent, General Johnston.

During his campaign, Sherman freed more than 40,000 slaves, many of whom simply began to follow the Army into Savannah and the Carolinas. Alarmed by the responsibility to care for so many people, Sherman issued his Special Field Orders, Number 15. This provided newly released slaves with their own parcel of land, which Sherman had seized from white landowners.

After the war, when Grant was promoted to General of the Army, Sherman received a promotion to Lieutenant General (four stars). When Grant was elected president of the United States, he appointed Sherman the commanding general. For the next 15 years Sherman would oversee the Indian Wars that followed in the wake of the Civil War.

In later life Sherman often spoke of his hatred for war. He wrote, "Tis only those who have never heard a shot, never heard the shriek and groans of the wounded and lacerated . . . that cry aloud for more blood, more vengeance, more desolation." Sherman is also credited with the famous phrase, "War is hell."

William T. Sherman died on February 14, 1891, in New York City. After a military procession there, his body was sent to St. Louis, Missouri, where his son, Thomas Ewing Sherman, a Jesuit priest, provided his father's funeral Mass.

Marilyn Monroe

Legendary American Movie Star
(June 1, 1926 - August 5, 1962)

Marilyn Monroe

"Life –

"I am of both your directions …

"Strong as the cobwebs in the wind." *(p. 141)*

Taken From Marilyn Monroe: a life of the actress by Carl Edmund Rollyson Ann Arbor, Mich: UMI Research Press, 1986.

"As long as I can remember, I've always loved people." (p.12)

Taken From Marilyn: Her Life in Her Own Words: Marilyn Monroe's Revealing Last Words… by George Barris; Kensington Publishing Corp., New York, 1995.

Even today, the death of Marilyn Monroe at the young age of 36 remains shrouded in mystery. Her life—often contradictory and lived in public view—offers an equal air of mystery.

The world knew her as a beautiful but ditzy blonde bombshell. Certainly, she portrayed this image in many movies. For many she symbolized female perfection. She was an icon, the ultimate representation of feminine allure.

Yet, those who knew her best suspected a much more complex intelligence, offset by a deep running insecurity and vulnerability that shadowed every step of her life. Jane Russell, her co-star in *Gentlemen Prefer*

Blondes and one of Marilyn's best friends, described her as shy, sweet, and intelligent, the last characteristic not well known to people who did not know her very well. After directing her in the movie *Bus Stop,* Joshua Logan paid homage to her great talent and bright mind.

She was born on June 1, 1926, at the Los Angeles County Hospital. Her mother, Gladys Pearl Baker, named her Norma Jean. She never knew the true identity of her father.

A "rollercoaster" would be the mildest term to describe Norma Jean's childhood and adolescence. Instability proved the only constant in her life. Her mother's lack of mental or emotional stability manifested itself shortly after her birth. Norma Jean went to live with foster parents, Albert and Ida Bolender.

When Norma Jean was seven, her mother purchased a home and retrieved the little girl to come live with her. Within a few months, Gladys suffered a nervous breakdown and was forcibly removed to the State Hospital in Norwalk.

After being named a ward of the state, Norma Jean acquired a legal guardian in the person of her mother's best friend, Grace McKee. Two years later, Grace married Ervin Goddard and turned Norma Jean over to the Los Angeles Orphan's Home.

Norma Jean found herself bounced among a series of foster homes. While several families considered formal adoption, her mother's refusal to sign the adoption papers frustrated those efforts. She landed with her aunt Ana Lower. With her aunt's health deteriorating, she returned to live with Grace and her family for a short period.

Within months, Grace and her husband decided to move to Virginia. As a matter of convenience, Grace approached a neighbor and suggested that Norma Jean, still under legal age, marry the woman's son, James Dougherty, so that Norma Jean would not have to return to the orphanage or to foster care. The two young people already knew each other. They were married in June 1942.

In 1943, in the midst of World War II, Jim Dougherty enlisted in the Merchant Marines. Like many women during the war years, Norma Jean sought employment with the war effort. She worked at the Radioplane Munitions Factory, but she also joined a modeling agency without telling her husband.

Jim first became aware of her modeling career when a shipmate showed him her picture in a magazine. Returning from the war, Jim voiced a strong opposition to her modeling, but she refused to quit. They were divorced in 1946.

Her modeling success impressed Ben Lyon of 20th Century Fox. He arranged for a screen test and influenced her decision to change her name. She quickly progressed from uncredited roles to minor speaking parts. For the next few years she played low budget films with small parts in higher caliber films.

For much of her career Monroe played the

scatterbrained blonde in comedies, the woman who could make men's heads spin but who could barely unlock the door for herself. She protected her image as the female all men wanted to protect rather than a woman who could take part in a serious conversation.

It was only later in her career, when she proved that she could carry big budget films, that her native intelligence began to emerge. She organized her own production company and began forcing movie executives to allow her to play stronger, more intelligent women.

Just as she was beginning to hit her stride as a major actress, she fell in love with and married baseball's all-time great Joe DiMaggio on January 14, 1954. The media world acclaimed the duo as the perfect couple. But this marriage lasted less than a year. DiMaggio had hoped for a more traditional wife; Monroe was beginning to achieve stardom. The conflict shattered their marriage, although his love for her remained untarnished for the rest of his life.

Finally, by the mid-1950s, industry insiders began to recognize her not simply as a comedic sex symbol but as a serious dramatic actress. After her performance in the movie *Bus Stop*, critics were stunned. Many did not hesitate to bestow the highest compliments. Even the great actor Laurence Olivier said of her performance in *The Prince and the Showgirl* that her comedy was brilliant, performed with dramatic skill.

She won a Golden Globe award for best actress

in *Some Like It Hot.* She received the Italian equivalent of an Academy Award, the David di Donatello, and the French Crystal Star Award for *The Prince and the Showgirl.*

On June 29, 1956, Monroe married the famous playwright Arthur Miller. This third and final marriage spanned the most successful and turbulent years of her career. The marriage failed in fewer than five years, a little more than a year before her death. His comments on their time together contain some of his greatest creative imagery and beautiful prose.

Although Marilyn Monroe seemed to race through her life, her career, and her marriages, ironically, the main complaint voiced by nearly all of her co-stars was that she was consistently late for everything. Sir Laurence Olivier was reportedly furious during the shooting of the *Prince and the Showgirl* for her habit of being late to the set.

During the shooting of *The Misfits,* which became both Clark Gable's as well as Marilyn Monroe's last completed film, she continued with her tardy habit. This infuriated Gable. Some newspapers blamed the stress created by Monroe when Gable died of a heart attack shortly after filming.

Ironically, much of her tardiness evolved from her extreme stage fright. Throughout her career, simply arriving at the set required a gallant effort. Despite her popularity and critical acclaim, her insecurity took a heavy toll.

Marilyn Monroe died on August 5, 1962, at the

age of 36. Her death remains a mystery. Elton John sang a famous tribute to her life and death many years later, "Candle in the Wind." It is a haunting song of lost potential.

She was buried in the Westwood Village Memorial Park Cemetery in Los Angeles, California. Earlier that year Joe DiMaggio had asked her to remarry him. He claimed her body and arranged for her funeral. For the next 20 years he sent a half-dozen red roses to her burial place three times a week.

Leo Tolstoy

Russian Novelist
(August 28, 1828 – November 20, 1910)

Leo Tolstoy

"If I am a Christian, then the law of vengeance is replaced by the law of love…" *(p. 52)*

"The good cannot seize power, nor retain it; to do this, men must love power. And the love of power is inconsistent with goodness; but quite consistent with the very opposite qualities – pride, cunning, cruelty." *(p. 85)*

Taken from "The Kingdom of God is within you": CHRISTIANITY NOT AS A MYSTIC RELIGION BUT AS A NEW THEORY OF LIFE. Volume II. Translated from the Russian of Count Leo Tolstoy by Constance Garnett, London; William Heinermann (1894).

Of all the great literary figures of history, Count Leo Tolstoy looks the most like a mad Russian revolutionary, with a shaggy spray of grey-white beard that appears to bristle with indignation. His overarching eyebrows, thick forehead, and angry eyes all enhance the look of icy rage, as if he could barely restrain the impulse to attack the Tsar's palace.

In reality, and in contrast with his fierce appearance, Tolstoy was a fervent Christian. He believed in a literal interpretation of Christ's ethical teachings, especially the Sermon on the Mount. His writings and personal example of nonviolent resistance greatly influenced both Mahatma Gandhi in India and Martin Luther

King Jr. in the United States, early in their lifelong crusades for justice and equality.

As a novelist, Tolstoy was a proponent of realistic fiction, a school of thought that used the novel form merely as a tool for exploring issues of the time, such as social conditions and political philosophy as well as current governments. He initially wrote both *War and Peace* and *Anna Karenina*, two of his most famous works, as realist exercises, but later he rejected the idea that they achieved his original aims.

Nearly all of the world's greatest writers and literary critics acknowledge Tolstoy as one of Russia's finest writers. Instead of the usual pattern of an older writer coming under criticism for adhering to an outmoded style, Tolstoy in his old age enjoyed great acclaim from the young, up-and-coming writers who became very famous themselves, such as Virginia Woolf, James Joyce, Anton Chekhov, Marcel Proust, and William Faulkner. He continues to garner acclaim from literary critics, writers, and academics, even today.

Despite Tolstoy's lifelong criticism of Russian aristocracy, even the Tsar took a personal interest in him. When Tolstoy fought for Russia in the Crimean War, Tsar Alexander II ordered his troops to "guard well the life of that man."

Leo Tolstoy was born to Russian nobility on August 28, 1828, in central Russia. The grandest families of Russian aristocracy claimed a family relationship with the Tolstoys.

His mother died when he was two years old. He was only nine years old when he lost his father. In later years he immortalized both of his parents as characters in his novels.

Although wealthy and of noble birth, Leo enlisted as a private in an artillery unit in the Crimean War to fight for Imperial Russia against France, Britain, and the Ottoman Empire. He was quickly promoted to lieutenant. His experience in the war provided him with the material for his novel *The Cossacks*, considered by many to be the best story ever written in the Russian language.

Throughout his life Tolstoy was torn between the privileges of his aristocratic birth and the plight of the peasants. He came to believe he was undeserving of his wealth and inherited station in life. Frequently, he gave large amounts of money to street beggars when he visited the large cities of Russia. On his own country estate he was known among the peasantry for his generosity.

In later years his search for moral stability continued to torment him. He attempted to rid himself of his wealth and even surrendered much of his land to the people. He renounced the copyrights to many of his works.

Most of his family, especially his wife, turned against him because of this. She refused to give up her possessions. Asserting her obligation to provide for their large family, she forced Tolstoy to give her the copyrights of his earlier writing. Because of his inability to compromise his new-found belief system, and because of her inability to accept poverty on behalf of herself and their children, the Tolstoys allowed their marriage to disintegrate into an unhappy coexistence for the last decade before Leo Tolstoy's death.

As much a philosopher as a writer in his elder years, he supported the doctrine of civil disobedience espoused by Henry David Thoreau, the celebrated American philosopher. He also promoted nonviolence to such a degree that the great Indian spiritual leader, Mahatma Gandhi, became devoted to his teachings on the subject.

When he was 82 years old, his desire to reject all material possessions began to overwhelm him. Even the care provided by his wife and daughters, who kept his ill health from becoming worse, became too much of a burden and he left home. He decided to wander throughout Russia with only the company of his younger daughter, Alexandra, and his doctor.

Only a few days after leaving home, on November 20, 1910, Tolstoy was overcome by fever at the Astapovo train station. He never left the station. Overcome by pneumonia, he died several days later. He was buried in a peasant's grave and thousands of peasants lined the street at his funeral.

Maya Angelou

American Author, Poet, Dancer, Actor, Civil Rights Activist
(April 4, 1928 – Present)

Maya Angelou

"We, the black people, the most displaced, the poorest, the most maligned and scourged, we had the glorious task of reclaiming the soul and saving the honor of the country. We, the most hated, must take hate into our hands and by the miracle of love, turn loathing into love. We the most feared and apprehensive, must take fear and by love, change it into hope. We now die daily in large and small ways, must take the demon death and turn it into life." *(p. 69)*

Taken From The Heart of a Woman by Maya Angelou. Published by Random House, New York; 1981.

Maya Angelou was born a year before the Stock Market Crash of 1929. For the next twelve years, families saw their dreams shattered by the Great Depression, the worst economic collapse in American history. From toddler to teenager Maya grew up at a time when the vast majority of Americans struggled just to feed their families.

Life provided few opportunities for a black, female child. She was the wrong gender in a male-dominated society and the wrong color in a racially divided country. To make matters worse, she was molested at eight years of age by a man she trusted. For the next five years she refused to speak a word.

Somehow she found the courage to turn the

terrible hardships of her youth into a life dedicated to championing the weak and oppressed. She spoke with forceful conviction for those without a voice in their society.

On February 15, 2011—at the age of 83—Maya Angelou received the Presidential Medal of Freedom, the nation's highest civilian honor. Speaking before the award ceremony, she reflected on her personal history as well as the history of slavery and freedom from slavery, stating that it reminded her of who she was, of how proud she was to be who she was. She honored every person who had ever come to America in her speech, and she claimed her Medal of Freedom in the name and for the honor of all people seeking freedom.

People around the world wept to see her receive the Medal. But few were surprised. Beginning in 1973, many of America's most prestigious universities have awarded Maya Angelou with nearly 40 honorary degrees. During her wide-ranging career she received a Pulitzer Prize nomination for her poetry and a Tony Award nomination for her acting. She was awarded three Grammys for her spoken word albums.

She was born Marguerite Ann Johnson to parents Bailey and Vivian Johnson in St. Louis, Missouri, on April 4, 1928. Her older brother gave her the nickname "Maya." She created the stage name Maya Angelou when she worked at The Purple Onion in 1952, a San Francisco nightclub.

When Maya was three, her parents' marriage

collapsed. Her father placed her and her brother (age 4) on a train by themselves and sent them to live with his mother, Annie Henderson, in Stamps, Arkansas. Four years later, without warning, he came to Stamps to take the children to live with their mother in St. Louis.

In St. Louis, Maya's mother's boyfriend, Mr. Freeman, molested Maya. Although convicted of the crime, the boyfriend spent only one day in jail. Four days after his release the police discovered his murdered body. For the next five years Maya became mute, never speaking a word.

Many years later she explained her silence. At her young age she thought that by telling people the name of her abuser, her voice had killed the man. She feared that if she spoke again her voice could kill others.

Shortly after Mr. Freeman's murder, she and her brother were returned to their grandmother, whom she called Mamma. While the adults in her life began to wonder if she would ever speak again, Mamma—a deeply religious woman—assured her that the Good Lord would resolve her pain. The words would flow again. There were too many things the girl needed to tell the world.

Maya went to live with her mother in San Francisco at age 13. Some years later as a young woman with a small son, her life began a downward spiral. Survival forced her to make hard choices that could have damaged her future permanently. Instead she chose to utilize this "wilderness period" to define herself and become the woman her grandmother envisioned.

Eventually, Angelou won a scholarship to study dance. The great modern dance artist Martha Graham became a teacher and mentor. Angelou toured Europe with the Gershwin brothers' American folk opera, *Porgy and Bess.*

Near the end of the 1950s Angelou moved to New York City to act in off-Broadway shows, and there she met people who were active in the civil rights movement. After meeting Martin Luther King Jr. in 1960, she joined the civil rights movement. In 1964, Angelou met Malcolm X in Ghana, Africa, and they became good friends. She returned with him to the United States to help him build the Organization of African American Unity. The assassinations of both men, Malcolm X in 1965, and Martin Luther King Jr. in 1968, devastated her.

Yet, by the age of 40, Maya Angelou could look back on her life and see a remarkable transformation and evolution. She had navigated a long voyage from damaged child and destitute young woman to a massive list of achievements—singer, dancer, actor, civil rights activist, and more. The world valued her talents.

Her greatest legacy would be unveiled in 1969 with the publication of her autobiography *I Know Why the Caged Bird Sings.* The memoir recounted the first 17 years of her life. It rocketed her to international fame and was nominated for a National Book Award.

Over the years she added five more volumes to the chronicles of her life.

Maya Angelou created something remarkable with her series of memoirs, not just by recounting the stories of a black female. Her books told the unvarnished and—at times—unlovely truth. She held nothing back, left nothing hidden. This shocked and angered many people but encouraged many more to compare their life experiences with hers.

Few women have spoken more clearly or more forcefully for civil rights and the role of women in society, especially black women. Today, through her writing and commentary, Maya Angelou is widely acknowledged as a spokesperson for blacks and for women at every level of society, around the world.

Rudyard Kipling

British Poet and Writer
Nobel Laureate for Literature
(December 30, 1865 – January 18, 1936)

Rudyard Kipling

Poem (first stanza)

WHEN EARTH'S LAST PICTURE IS PAINTED

**When Earth's last picture is painted
and the tubes are twisted and dried,**

**When the oldest colours have faded,
and the youngest critic has died,**

**We shall rest, and, faith, we shall need it –
lie down for an aeon or two,**

**Till the Master of All Good Workmen
shall put us to work anew.** *(p. 73)*

*Taken from Kipling poems by Rudyard Kipling - selection by Peter
Washington. Published by Alfred A. Knopf, a division of Random House,
Inc. New York. Everyman's Library 2007.*

The stories, novels, and poems of Rudyard
Kipling have provided a literary base for children,
teenagers, and adults for more than a century. Even
Walt Disney paid tribute to Kipling's story-telling
genius in the animated movie *The Jungle Book*. Yet, long
before Disney artists applied paint to brush, millions
of children around the world already considered
themselves best friends with the jungle child Mowgli
and the animals who served as his foster parents. Lord
Baden-Powell utilized many of Kipling's jungle book

themes when he founded the Boy Scouts.

Nearly as popular were his *Just so Stories* in which Kipling developed an entire mythology about jungle creatures. In the original edition, the author personally illustrated such stories as *How the Camel Got Its Hump* and *How the Leopard Got Its Spots*.

Rudyard Kipling was born in Bombay, India, on December 30, 1865, the son of John and Alice Kipling. He describes his youngest years as a time of delight, when he spoke the native language of India, Hindi, more fluently than English. When he was five years old, as was the custom of the day, his parents took him and his younger sister, Alice, age 3, back to England and left them there.

Thus began one of the most horrible experiences of his life. His foster parents, Captain and Mrs. Holloway, subjected him to a regimen of cruelty and neglect. As he recounts in his autobiography, "I have known a certain amount of bullying, but this was calculated torture."

He found relief only in the times, such as Christmas, when he and his sister were sent to visit their mother's sister, Georgiana. He called these brief visits "a paradise which I verily believe saved me."

His mother returned to England when Rudyard was 12 years old and removed the children from the care of the Holloway family. When asked why he did not tell anyone about the horrible treatment, he responded, "Badly treated children have a clear notion of what they are likely to get if they betray the secrets of a prison house before they are clear of it."

Rudyard was then sent to a boarding school, more like a military academy, that prepared young men for university studies or a career in the armed forces. Toward the end of his residence, everybody decided he had better return to India, because he did not have the academic ability for a scholarship to Oxford University and he was not suited for military service. Accordingly, back he went to India to become the assistant editor of a small newspaper, *The Civil and Military Gazette*.

His employment as a reporter gave Kipling the opportunity to travel and experience the cultures and lifestyles of India's people, both the English rulers and native societies. In addition to his responsibilities as a reporter he began to write a large number of short stories. In less than nine months, 39 of the short stories were published in the paper.

Eventually, a dispute with the editors led to his dismissal from the newspaper. He sold the copyrights to his writing and put together enough money to travel back to England in style. This time he went the long way home, from Singapore to Hong Kong to Japan and then to San Francisco. He spent a great deal of time touring North America. He met Mark Twain, the great American writer, who left him awestruck.

Upon his return to England, to his great surprise, he discovered that he had become a celebrity. He decided to progress from short fiction to writing novels and continued to receive accolades for his writing.

To an outside observer it might appear that Rudyard Kipling lived a charmed life. However, it was at this time that he suffered a nervous breakdown. The doctors recommended a long sea voyage. He visited Africa, Australia, New Zealand, and back to India before returning to England. Extensive travel remained one of the constants in Kipling's life, especially as a young man. He found comfort in the diversity of places, cultures, and circumstances.

Married at the age of 26, Kipling and his wife moved to the United States and built a home in Vermont, where his wife's family lived. He relished the country atmosphere of the northeastern United States. He called it a healthy, "sane clean life."

It was in Vermont that the idea for the jungle books came to fruition almost as if the idea came from outside of his body. "After blocking out the main idea in my head," he said, "the pen took charge, and I watched it begin to write stories about Mowgli and the animals, which later grew into the *Jungle Books.*" This was also the time when he wrote the novel *Captains Courageous*, as well as a number of his most famous poems, including *Mandalay* and *Gunga Din*.

The Kipling family returned to England in 1896. Barely 30 years old, Kipling now found himself a famous man. He continued to write and to travel extensively.

In 1907, Rudyard Kipling was awarded the Nobel

Prize for literature. The prize citation read, in part, "in consideration of the power of observation, originality of imagination, virility of ideas and remarkable talent for narration which characterize the creations of this world-famous author." He was the first Englishman to receive the Nobel Prize.

Kipling was offered the position of British Poet Laureate. He did not accept this post, nor would he consider a knighthood. Historians still debate his reasons.

On January 18, 1936, at the age of 70, Rudyard Kipling died suddenly of a hemorrhage from a perforated ulcer. His ashes were buried in the Poets' Corner in Westminster Abbey, in good company with other British literary luminaries.

Benito Juarez

**Mexican Politician and Reformer.
Mexico's First and Only
Full-Blooded Indigenous President**
(March 21, 1806 – July 18, 1872)

Benito Juárez

"May true Religion flourish and may false Governments be destroyed!" *(p.7)*

Taken from A life of Benito Juarez, constitutional president of Mexico by Ulick Ralph Burke. Remington and Company, Limited; London, 1894.

"Senior Secretario, when a proposition contains a question of right and wrong, I want no advice. Needing no mentor for my conscience, you may leave the room." *(p. 281)*

Taken from The Passing of the Fourteen: Life, Love and War Among the Brigands and Guerillas of Mexico by Ransom Sutton. The Devin-Adair Company, New York, 1916.

Sometime in 1818, a 12-year-old boy marched along a dusty trail, in places not more than a goat path, in the state of Oaxaca, a mountainous area in southwest Mexico. He was a full-blooded member of the Zapotec, the native people of the area.

Benito Juárez walked alone on his first great journey.

There was no mistaking the gleam in his eyes, the great burning in his chest, the fire in his gut. Probably he was a little afraid as well. But a dream consumed his small body, a dream that was both fantastic and more than a little outrageous. He planned to change the world—or at least himself.

In truth, at this point in his life, his goals were fierce but a little fuzzy.

He certainly possessed the power to accomplish the first step of his plan—walk to the great city of Oaxaca from his village, San Pablo Guelatao. There he needed to find his sister, Maria Josefa, who worked as a cook in one of the great houses, so he could get something to eat once he arrived.

His plan was unrealistic on many levels. Everything else about his life worked against his grand strategy to become a great man, to make a proper place for himself in the world. By the time he was three, both his parents had died of diabetes. A few years later both grandparents died, leaving his uncle as his guardian. His uncle was a good man but poor and unable to offer the opportunities that Benito yearned to have for himself.

Benito was tough from working his entire young life in the corn fields and minding the sheep. His dark complexion had been burned even darker by the sun. He never received any formal education. He did not speak, read, or write Spanish—only the Zapotec language.

Benito was nobody's idea of a cuddly puppy. Mexico was a country controlled by people whose ancestors had arrived from Spain. *Los Conquistadores* had torn down several empires and established an empire themselves. Benito understood that he possessed little chance for success in such a world. This he surely understood, even so young.

Once in Oaxaca, Benito found sanctuary in the home of Antonio Maza, where his sister worked. He became an exceptional student. Both Don Antonio and Antonio Salanueva, a Franciscan layman, were so impressed with Benito that they arranged for him to attend the city seminary. They hoped he would become a priest.

Benito Juárez chose not to become a priest. He continued his education, graduating from the Institute of Science and Art in 1834 with a law degree. Seven years later the local governmental authorities appointed him a judge. Within six years he became the governor of the state of Oaxaca.

From the beginning, Juárez's politics were anti-church and liberal. Throughout his career, he would work to confiscate the vast treasuries and landholdings of the Catholic Church. He dedicated himself to protect the poorest Mexicans from the powerful and the wealthy. These activities brought him into direct confrontation with the conservatives.

In 1846, the United States declared war against Mexico, specifically to overthrow the Mexican president, Antonio López de Santa Anna. This was the same Santa Anna whose army attacked the Alamo in Texas. After the United States captured Mexico City, Santa Anna fled the country.

Juárez and the other liberals gained national power, but Santa Anna returned in 1853. He reestablished his conservative government and exiled the liberals, including Benito Juárez. Escaping safely from Mexico,

Juárez traveled to Cuba and then to New Orleans, where he worked in a cigar and cigarette factory.

Juárez returned to Mexico in 1854 to help with the liberal revolution, which recaptured the capitol. For the moment the liberals again gained the upper hand. Juárez was named Chief Justice of the Supreme Court.

In 1857, the government changed hands again, as the conservatives overthrew the liberals and the president resigned. Juárez was arrested but later released from prison. He retreated to the northern part of Mexico and declared himself president of Mexico. Mexican law recognized the Chief Justice as the next in line as the head of government.

Between the years of 1858 to 1861, the liberals and conservatives fought the Reform War. With the defeat of the conservatives, Juárez returned to Mexico City and assumed the presidency of a united Mexico.

Unfortunately, The Reform War devastated the country economically. Juárez and his government defaulted on the money owed to foreign nations. Britain, Spain, and France sent troops to collect. Britain and Spain later pulled their troops from Mexico when they realized the French had imperialistic plans. France named Maximilian von Habsburg, an Austrian nobleman, as the Emperor of Mexico, under the authority of French emperor Napoleon III.

This created another war in Mexico. The Mexicans won their first great victory against the French on May 5, 1862 at Puebla. This day is still celebrated today as Cinco de Mayo. The French, however, ultimately won and established Maximilian as Emperor with a conservative government to rule in Mexico City.

The liberals, under Juárez, turned for help to the United States, and kept fighting. Maximilian was captured and executed in 1867. Benito Juárez was reelected to the presidency. He died of a heart attack while working at his office on July 18, 1872.

A few years after his death, his political enemy Porfirio Díaz took over the presidency. Effectively he turned the government into a dictatorship that lasted for three and a half decades, until the beginning of the Mexican Revolution in 1910.

As he fought to attain freedom for his countrymen, Benito Juárez failed and succeeded many times during his life—as a lawyer, judge, state governor, Chief Justice and President. He desired to change Mexico from a semi-feudal society to one of democracy. To a great extent he succeeded. History honors Benito Juárez as the Mexican Abraham Lincoln.

Phillis Wheatley

Slave and American Poet
(c. 1753 – December 5, 1784)

Phillis Wheatley

ON THE DEATH OF A YOUNG LADY
OF FIVE YEARS OF AGE

From dark abodes to fair ethereal light
Th' enraptured innocent has wing'd her flight;
On the kind bosom of eternal love
She finds unknown beatitude above.
This know, ye parents, nor her loss deplore,
She feels the iron hand of pain no more;
The dispensations of unerring grace,
Should turn your sorrows into grateful praise;
Let then no tears for her henceforward flow,
No more distress'd in our dark vale below. *(p. 24)*

TO THE REV. DR. THOMAS AMORY,
ON READING HIS SERMONS ON DAILY DEVOTIONS,
IN WHICH DUTY IS RECOMMENDED AND
ASSISTED.

To cultivate in ev'ry noble mind
Habitual grace, and sentiments refin'd,
Thus while you strive to mend the human heart,
Thus while the heav'nly precepts you impart,
O may each bosom catch the sacred fire,
And youthful minds to Virtue's throne aspire. *(p. 83)*

Taken from Poems on various subjects, religious and moral by Phillis Wheatley. Published according to Act of Parliament, Sept. 1, 1773 by Arch. d. Bell. Bookseller No. 8 near the Saracens head Aldgate.

Phillis Wheatley was a woman, a slave, and an

internationally celebrated poet. Such a combination in pre-revolutionary America defies calculation.

She was born somewhere in West Africa, likely in the area known today as the countries of The Gambia and Senegal, probably in 1753. Captured and enslaved around the age of seven, she was transported aboard the slave ship *The Phillis*. She arrived in Boston, Massachusetts, on July 11, 1761.

John Wheatley, a prominent Boston merchant, purchased her as a servant for his wife, Susanna. They named the young girl Phillis after the ship that had brought her to America.

Throughout the nearly 200-year history of slavery in the American Colonies and the United States, society discouraged the education of slaves. In most areas the law forbade teaching a slave to read. The people of the time believed that an educated slave might begin to think and act above their station in life.

The Wheatley family considered themselves among the most open-minded in Boston. Indeed, many people considered them exceptionally progressive for the time. Soon after Phillis arrived in the house, Mary, the Wheatley's 18-year-old daughter, began to tutor the bright young slave.

They were astonished by her ability to learn so quickly. With time they removed her from most household duties so that she could spend more time learning. They provided her with an education available to very few females at the time, let alone slaves.

Phillis began reading Greek and Latin classics

by the age of 12. Biblical passages became her daily recreation. She was heavily influenced by the writings and philosophies of some of the greatest literary men of that day—John Milton and Alexander Pope. In addition, she enjoyed the Greek and Latin classics by Homer, Horace, and Virgil. She began to produce poetry at an early age.

Honored by the Wheatley family as a curiosity but possibly given affection as well, Phillis was never allowed to completely bridge the gap between two absolutely distinct societies—master and slave. Not quite family, not quite slave, highly educated but still considered property. One can only imagine her inner thoughts and conflicts.

During the 1700s very few women published their writing. Those that did often published under a "pen name" or as "Anonymous." There were no female black writers or poets in the Americas, nor in Britain. Phillis was the first and only one of her kind. Before the age of 20, Phillis had received wide recognition in the Colonies.

Such was the astonishment among white Americans that in 1772 Phillis Wheatley was forced to defend her writing in court. A group of Boston's most prominent men, including John Irving, Reverend Charles Chauncey, John Hancock and the governor of Massachusetts sat in judgment.

They concluded that she truly wrote the poems by her own hand. They signed a document to that fact, which became part of the preface of her book, *Poems on Various Subjects, Religious and Moral,* published in London. Here is an excerpt from one of her poems:

"Twas mercy brought me from my Pagan land,
Taught my benighted soul to understand
That there's a God, that there's a Saviour too:
Once I redemption neither sought nor knew.
Some view our sable race with scornful eye,
"Their colour is a diabolic die."
Remember, Christians, Negroes, black as Cain,
May be refin'd, and join th' angelic train."

In 1773, she was sent with the family's eldest son, Nathaniel Wheatley, to London. There, the aristocracy of Britain received her with great acclaim, and the collection of her poetry was published with the help of the Countess of Huntingdon and the Earl of Dartmouth.

Returning to the Colonies, she published a poem about George Washington, titled *To His Excellency, George Washington.* In appreciation, Washington invited her to his home. Thomas Paine published the poem in the *Pennsylvania Gazette.*

Phillis Wheatley supported the American War of Independence. Still, the revolutionary fervor that swept through the Colonies proved unfavorable to her ability to publish her poetry. The passion for the revolution turned people away from poetry.

In 1778, her master, John Wheatley, died. She was legally emancipated from all bonds of slavery. Within three months she married a black freeman named John Peters, a grocer.

They lived in the worst conditions of poverty. Two of their children died in infancy. In 1784, her husband was imprisoned for debt and she became a scullery maid in a boarding house, washing pots and pans and doing the heavy work required in the kitchen.

Ground down by her circumstances and caring for a sickly baby, the hard work ravaged her health. She died a few months later, on December 5, 1784. Within a few hours, her infant son died as well.

In her day, many people acknowledged that Phillis Wheatley was well-educated and intelligent. Still, some of her admirers accepted her poetry primarily as a novelty. Yet, her poetry shows levels of subtlety and genius that are appreciated even today among scholars and fellow poets.

Phillis Wheatley filled her poetry with Christian imagery and elements from the classics of literature. On the surface they were often bright and full of praise for famous personalities of her time, and of history. Beneath the surface were layers of complexity unrealized by many of her contemporary readers.

Franz Joseph Haydn

Austrian Classical Composer
(March 31, 1732 – May 31, 1809)

Franz Joseph Haydn

"I listened more than I studied… Thus little by little my knowledge and my ability were developed." *(p.13)*

"I was set apart from the world, there was nobody in my vicinity to confuse and annoy me in my course, and so I had to be original." *(p. 34)*

Taken from Joseph Haydn; AN ESSENTIAL GUIDE TO HIS LIFE AND WORKS by Neil Wenborn. Pavilion Books Limited, London, 1997.

The great Austrian composer Joseph Haydn began his long career in humble circumstances. He was born to a poor family in a remote hamlet near the Hungarian border.

Known today as the "Father of the Symphony" and the "Father of the String Quartet," in the 18th century his popularity equaled a modern rock star or rap artist. He grew rich in an era when musicians were poor and dependent on the wealthy for patronage.

Along the way he worked for a prince—several, actually. He called Wolfgang Amadeus Mozart a personal friend. He was a teacher to Ludwig van Beethoven (though neither liked the other).

Born to a wheelwright father (a man who makes and repairs wagon wheels) and a mother who cooked for Count Harrach and his household, Joseph showed an early gift for music. Hoping to encourage his talent, his parents handed their six-year-old son to the church choirmaster in Hainburg, some miles away. He never returned to live with his family.

Joseph remembered his time at Hainburg primarily for the near-starvation diet and the shame he experienced because of his poor clothes. He did, however, learn the rudiments of the violin and the harpsichord. Within two years his high, clear voice earned him a position in the choir at St. Stephen's Cathedral in Vienna, which was a choir known throughout the land.

He remained at St. Stephen's until the age of 17 when his voice deepened and his inability to sing high choral parts diminished his value. After a prank that involved cutting off the pigtail of a fellow choir member, he was beaten and thrown out into the street. Fortunately, a friend's family took him into their home for a few months.

Thus began Haydn's time as a freelance artist. During this difficult period, he worked at anything that would put food in his mouth. For a while he was a music teacher and then a street performer. Finally, he landed a job as the personal attendant and keyboard accompanist for the Italian composer Nicola Porpora. From Porpora he learned the basics of music composition in which, up to that time, he had lacked training.

By the time Haydn was 21, he realized he needed more training in music theory. He soaked in every bit of knowledge from whatever source he could. In essence he taught himself what he lacked.

At every step along the path, whether singing in the boys' choir or freelancing to make ends meet, he continued to gain a reputation. Often he discovered his music being copied and sold without his receiving a fee. He shrugged this off as part of the learning process.

At the age of 28, Haydn found his first full-time job as the music director for Count Morzin. At this time he married, but very soon both he and his wife, Maria Anna, realized that they were trapped in an unhappy marriage. Unable to divorce under the laws of that time, they lived separate lives and had no children.

When the Count discharged Haydn, Prince Paul Anton wasted no time offering him employment with the Esterhazy family. Within a few years Haydn was the musical director for this grand, wealthy family. Nearly overwhelmed with the huge workload, he produced a flood of musical compositions and began to blossom.

Haydn worked for the Esterhazy princes for about 30 years. During that time he became extremely famous, even though he never left the Esterhazy household. Haydn was 54 in 1790 when Prince Anton became the head of the household. To reduce expenses, the prince severely reduced Haydn's salary but gave him permission to travel the world.

This proved to be the turning point in Joseph

Haydn's life. He had always felt isolated in the Esterhazy household, far from the great music center of Vienna and the rest of the world. Now his opportunity had arrived.

Haydn journeyed to England. The English aristocracy and the public at large received Haydn as if he were visiting nobility. He flourished during his first visit from 1791 to 1792, and again from 1794 to 1795. It was during these visits that he composed some of his greatest works.

On his return to Austria, he again took up his work for the Esterhazy family. However, he spent most of his time in Vienna, at his own home. Now in his 60s, his health began to decline. Growing old frustrated Haydn. Although he had many ideas for new compositions in his mind, his failing body made it more and more difficult to perform the arduous task of composing on paper.

On March 27, 1808, the premier musicians of Austria organized a final tribute in his honor. In his mid-70s and frail, all of Vienna and Austria considered him the grand master of music. Although greatly moved, he was so exhausted that he departed at intermission.

A few days before Haydn's death in 1809, Napoleon's army attacked Vienna. During the attack, as the cannons roared in the distance and his frightened servants gathered around him, he said, "My children, have no fear, for where Haydn is, no harm can fall."

Ingrid Bergman

Swedish Actress & Film Star
(August 29, 1915 – August 29, 1982)

Ingrid Bergman

"Tell me, please tell me, why at that first audition did you treat me so badly?... Alf stared at me as if I'd gone mad. 'Disliked you so much! Dear girl, you're crazy! The minute you leapt out of the wings onto the stage, and stood there laughing at us, we turned around and said to each other, 'Well, we don't have to listen to her, she's in! Look at that security. Look at that stage presence. Look at that impertinence. You jumped out onto the stage like a tigress." *(p 16)*

"The contrast between my acting exhibitions and my normal behavior was so different that it was unbelievable. I was the shyest human being ever invented. I couldn't come into a room without bumping into the furniture and then blushing..." *(p. 27)*

"Suddenly he became very quiet. He looked at me very hard, and he said, 'I've got an idea that's so simple and yet no one in Hollywood has ever tried it before. Nothing about you is going to be touched. Nothing altered. You remain yourself. You are going to be the first "natural actress..." *(pp. 68-69)*

Taken from Ingrid Bergman – My Story by Ingrid Bergman and Alan Burgess. Delacorte Press, New York; 1980.

As a rule actors (male or female) rarely become stars. Even if they develop into experts at their craft, perhaps geniuses at becoming the characters they play, most never reach the exalted level where their faces stare out at supermarket shoppers from shiny magazines lined up at the checkout counter.

On the other hand, the celebrated handful of actors who achieve the status of movie star routinely discover that their enormous success overpowers the characters they play. Their faces—their very lifestyles—are so well known that their performances never totally disappear into their characters. Still, they are beloved by audiences.

Ingrid Bergman managed to become both a superb actor and a great star. And she made it appear almost effortless. From the beginning of her acting career she set the screen on fire while managing to become the essence of whatever character she played on the big silver screen.

In her lifetime she was nominated for seven Academy Awards and won three times. She also won three Golden Globes, two Emmy Awards for television performances, and a Tony Award for stage acting, all for Best Actress. She spoke five languages fluently—Swedish (her native tongue), German, French, Italian, and English. She acted in movies in all five languages.

Born in Stockholm, Sweden, on August 29, 1915, when Ingrid was three years old her mother died. She developed an extremely close relationship with her father until he passed away when she was 12. After her father's death, she was raised by relatives.

An artist, her father always wanted to paint her portrait, but he was never able to accomplish the task. She was a restless girl and would not slow down long enough to pose for the painting. In later years she listed this as one of her regrets in life, saying, "I am sorry now, but I am one of those people who simply can't sit down and do nothing."

At the age of 17 she auditioned for the Royal Dramatic Theatre in Stockholm. She left the audition devastated, thinking she had failed miserably. Later, the faculty told her that she had performed so brilliantly that they knew immediately that she would get the position. They decided they didn't need to see anything more she could do, and that was why her audition was very short compared to some of the other students' auditions.

Within a year a Swedish film company hired her and she left the Royal Dramatic Theatre. She would make a dozen films in Sweden and one in Germany before being discovered by the famous Hollywood producer David O. Selznick.

Selznick urged her to change her name as many Hollywood actors did at the time. He thought she should have her teeth capped and her eyebrows plucked. He wanted her to submit to the care of professional makeup artists. Bergman refused to do any of these things. She insisted that she remain as he found her. Stunned by her refusal, Selznick allowed her to keep her real name and her natural features.

Bergman became a star with her first Selznick production, titled *Intermezzo*. Hollywood immediately recognized her beauty and talent. In addition, she brought a regal, natural appearance that contrasted sharply with the artificiality of the film industry. Her unpainted fingernails and unfussy cosmetics served her better than a flock of beauticians.

Although in later years she became more and more famous for her starring role opposite Humphrey Bogart in the movie *Casablanca*, she preferred more serious movies. She explained that as a Swede, she was a member of a serious-minded race whose rugged country and climate had developed in them a natural gravity and aversion to frivolity. Therefore she liked serious parts in movies more than parts requiring her simply to play the love interest.

In American minds the image of Ingrid Bergman became the polar opposite of the glittering falseness and unrestraint of other Hollywood stars. She came to symbolize a larger-than-life moderation. Fellow cast members and film workers reported that she never threw tantrums. Between scenes she read quietly in her trailer.

Although people tried to put her on a pedestal, she never represented herself as anyone other than who she was, a normal human being who was also an actress. In 1949, Bergman went to Italy to work for Italian director Roberto Rossellini. Although married to others, during the making of the film they fell in love.

This created a huge scandal in the United States. Condemned in every corner, Bergman was even denounced in the United States Senate. Ed Sullivan disinvited her to be on his television show. Leaving her husband and daughter in the United States, Bergman fled to Europe, eventually marrying Rossellini. The marriage lasted only seven years while Bergman made films in Italy.

In 1956 she returned to the American screen, starring in *Anastasia*. She won the Academy Award for best actress for that role. Her good friend Cary Grant accepted her Oscar since Bergman declined appearing.

For the rest of her career she alternated her performances among American films, European films, stage work, and television.

In 1974, Bergman won her third and final Academy Award for best supporting actress for her performance in *Murder on the Orient Express*.

At the end of her life, she starred in a television drama about Israeli Prime Minister Golda Meier for which she won both a Golden Globe and an Emmy. Both awards were given to her posthumously.

Ingrid Bergman died on August 29, 1982, in London, England, which was her 67th birthday. In accordance with her wishes, her cremated ashes were partially scattered in the sea and the rest were buried next to her parents in Stockholm, Sweden.

Stonewall Jackson

Confederate General – American Civil War
(January 21, 1824 – May 10, 1863)

Stonewall Jackson

"I know that I shall have the application necessary to succeed. I hope that I have the capacity. At least I am determined to try, and I wish you to help me to do this." Jackson's response to a deflating interview for West Point. He was admitted shortly thereafter." *(p.25)*

"Do your duty." *(p. 749)*

"I see from the number of physicians that you think my condition is dangerous, but I thank God, if it is His will, that I am ready to go. I am not afraid to die." *(p. 749)*

Taken from Stonewall Jackson – THE MAN, THE SOLDIER, THE LEGEND; by James I Robertson, Jr. Published by Macmillan Publishing, New York, 1997.

In the depth of darkness on May 2, 1863, nervous Confederate sentries on picket duty in rural Virginia fired into a group of mounted men. It was a mistake that altered history.

Rather than a marauding squadron of Union Cavalry, the horsemen consisted of four-star Lieutenant General Thomas Jonathan "Stonewall" Jackson and his command staff. They were returning from their brilliant victory over elements of the Union army at Chancellorsville.

Several staff officers were killed. Frantic, the group attempted to identify themselves, to which Major John

D. Barry of the 18th North Carolina Infantry replied, "It's a damned Yankee trick! Fire!"

In the second volley, three bullets entered the general's body, two in the left arm and one through his right hand. Within hours surgeons removed Jackson's left arm.

A horrified General Robert E. Lee sent a message, "Could I have directed events, I would have chosen for the good of the country to be disabled in your stead."

Days later General Stonewall Jackson died of complications. In the Civil War even simple wounds often resulted in death because of primitive surgical practices and infections.

Within the established genres of literary fiction, military fiction owns a small niche with an intensely devoted readership. Within the category of military fiction resides a favored cubbyhole known as "alternative history." Alternative history consists of unanswerable questions. What if Stonewall Jackson had lived?

The great battle of Gettysburg, fought less than two months after Jackson's death, turned the tide of war against the South. It could have gone either way. General Jackson, a much better tactician than most of the generals who fought that battle on either side, might have managed a Southern victory. If Stonewall Jackson had lived and fought at Gettysburg, the map of the United States might be very different today.

Thomas Jonathan Jackson entered the world on

January 21, 1824. He was barely a toddler when his father, a lawyer, died of typhoid fever. His mother, Julia, paid the debts and took in sewing and also taught school to support herself and her three remaining children.

When Thomas was six, his mother married Blake Woodson, also a lawyer. Thomas and his siblings were sent to live with various relatives within months of the marriage. A year after the marriage, Julia died after giving birth to Thomas's half-brother. Seven-year-old Thomas and five-year-old Laura went to live with their father's brothers; their older brother, Warren, went to relatives of their mother.

Raised in the frontier regions of Virginia, Thomas was mostly self-taught. At one point he made a deal with a young slave to exchange reading lessons for a supply of pine knots. Thomas burned the pine knots at night to read the books he borrowed. He attempted to attend school whenever he could, which was not often.

Thomas began formal schooling in 1842 at the United States Military Academy at West Point, New York. Because of his lack of formal education he found the work very difficult. Yet the iron self-discipline that would characterize his entire life moved him from the bottom of the class. By 1846 when he graduated, he was ranked 17th out of 59.

After graduation Jackson fought in the Mexican-American War, from 1846 to 1848. Beginning as a second lieutenant of artillery, Jackson eventually reached the temporary battlefield rank of major by the end of the war. The army commander Winfield Scott noted that Jackson had earned more promotions than any other officer during the three-year war.

Three years later he changed careers, at least partly, when he began teaching at the Virginia Military Academy (VMI). He was a professor of Natural and Experimental Philosophy, and he taught artillery. Still today many of his artillery tactics are taught at VMI.

He was not, however, a particularly good teacher. He possessed a rigid and authoritarian personality. He considered the inability to learn from his lectures a form of insubordination that merited punishment. His students disliked and even feared him to the extent that a group of his former students attempted to have him removed from the institution.

Before the beginning of the Civil War in 1861, the Virginia governor, John Fletcher, ordered Jackson to take command of Harpers Ferry. Jackson raised a brigade and became known for his strict discipline and the relentless drilling of his troops.

He acquired the name "Stonewall" at the first battle of Bull Run. Upon seeing Jackson's troops approaching his struggling troops, Brigadier General Barnard Elliott Bee Jr. said, "There is Jackson standing like a stone wall. Let us determine to die here, and we will conquer. Rally behind the Virginians!"

Jackson gained fame in the Valley campaign of 1862. When the Army of the Potomac under Union General George B. McClellan marched on the Confederate capital at Richmond, Jackson met the part of McClellan's forces attacking through the Shenandoah Valley. The Union Army in the Shenandoah contained more than 60,000 men. Jackson defeated them with a combined force of 17,000 men.

He accomplished this extraordinary feat of military prowess by attacking the Federal army as individual elements, where he held the advantage of numbers. He forced his infantry to move so fast that the Union generals believed that Jackson commanded an army much larger than their own. This earned his small army the nickname "the foot cavalry." He became a hero throughout the South.

General Jackson was a straightforward and hard-edged man. He lacked the gentle courtesies often expected of a Confederate general, and his uniforms were notoriously worn looking. He even wore his battle uniform to formal functions.

Before the battle of Fredericksburg, Major General Jeb Stewart, one of the most fashionable Confederate generals, presented Jackson with a finely tailored uniform. At the insistence of his staff, Jackson wore the beautiful uniform to a formal dinner. Soldiers rushed from every direction to see General Jackson in his finery. The humorless Jackson packed his elegant uniform away.

General Jackson attained one of his greatest victories in the battle of Chancellorsville. Jackson marched his men on the flanking move to the west of the Federal line and attacked the Union encampment while they were still eating breakfast. Many Union soldiers were captured without a shot. The rest fled the battlefield, pursued by Jackson's troops until dark.

Never one to waste any effort celebrating, Jackson ordered his command staff to accompany him back to his division. Within hours he would lie wounded and under the mercy of the surgeon's knife.

On the day of his death, May 10, 1863, General Jackson is quoted as saying, "It is the Lord's day; my wishes fulfilled. I have always desired to die on Sunday." General Jackson's last words were, "Let us cross over the river, and rest under the shade of the trees."

General Robert E. Lee mourned the loss of his friend and trusted commander. He told his cook, "William, I have lost my right arm."

James A. Michener

Bestselling American Author
(February 3, 1907 - October 16, 1997)

James A. Michener

"My life has been, in its way, sort of a fable for our times- a portrait of the American experience – a guy starting with absolutely nothing, winding up giving away a substantial fortune." *(p.2)*

"I never really had childhood ambitions. I've had reunions with people who knew me for a long time, and their testimony is overwhelmingly that they never expected much from me. They knew I was a bright guy but not very well organized." *(p. 8)*

"I went along fairly happily, though I was a very difficult child. I don't think I was very likeable. I never had any clothes that were bought for me until I was about fourteen. I never had a pair of skates or sneakers, never had a bicycle, never had a little wagon or a baseball glove. I never had an automobile or the use of an automobile. Never took vacations. And I used to get into fights. Look at my nose, it goes around a corner. That's from speaking when I should have been listening." *(p. 9-10)*

Taken from Talking with Michener by Lawrence Grobel and James Albert Michener. University Press of Mississippi; 1ˢᵗ ed (1999).

Long before the *Twilight* novels, long before Harry Potter and Hogwarts were heard of, the fiction of James Michener ruled popular literature. For more than 45 years, from the late 1940s to the 1990s, the news that another Michener novel was about to be released brought a shiver of anticipation to anyone who enjoyed a good read.

People began to count down the days. The minute his new book hit the shelves, bookstores, both large and small, built massive displays. Long lines would circle the block long before the bookstores opened their doors. Unlike today, casual wear at book parties did not include witch or vampire costumes.

Michener loved to travel and experience different cultures, foods, religions, and languages. He once said it would be better to stay home otherwise. As a result, he invested months digging deep into the history and lifestyles of the area where he set each book. He was never timid about sharing what he discovered with his readers.

In the novel *Hawaii* (1959), his opening pages describe the undersea volcanoes that created the islands, then the novel moves forward in time to the first Polynesians, then the white Christian missionaries, and finally World War II. His novel *Centennial* (1974), set in Colorado, begins with the dinosaurs who roamed the area. *Chesapeake* (1978) opens with the original Native Americans who settled the great bay that touches modern-day Virginia and Maryland.

During his nine decades of living, James never knew his real parents. In later life he counted this a blessing. He would say that he could be a genetic mix of anything. He regarded a mix of spiritual heritages as his own.

As an abandoned baby born in 1907, James grew

up in extreme poverty. He was raised by a Quaker widow named Mabel Michener, in Doylestown, Pennsylvania. She took in homeless children and there were sometimes eight or nine children in the house. All she could give him was love. To his dying day he called her Mother.

The lack of material possessions impacted James in a profound way. He remembered at Christmas he never received the special gifts his classmates took for granted. As a result he came to the conclusion that money would never be a motivation in his life. From that point forward, money never mattered to him and he did not worry about it.

In his mid-teens he decided to ramble around the country. It was a much simpler time in America, the 1920s. Along the way he traveled by any means available, hitchhiking or hopping a ride on a freight train. He earned money doing any job available. Between each trip he returned home for a time. Before he was 20 he had visited all but three states in the continental United States.

At first he thought that the people he encountered would be the same as those in Bucks County, Pennsylvania, where he grew up. While the scenery might change, he assumed that each community was a reproduction of the small town people from home.

Gradually he began to understand that each of the places and the people were different. He met black sharecroppers in the cotton shacks of Georgia. He made friends in the Hispanic communities in Colorado.

Each contained cultures completely different from the small community where he was raised.

Those travels formed the foundation of his lifelong love of other places. The profound realization that the world provided a nearly endless variety of peoples and cultures changed something deep inside him.

He attended Swarthmore College as a scholarship student and found his niche in research and teaching. He graduated with the highest honors—summa cum laude. He taught high school for a few years and studied in Europe for two more. He earned a master's degree at Colorado State Teachers college.

At age 34 at the beginning of World War II, Michener served as a lieutenant in the United States Navy. He traveled throughout the Pacific Theatre of War and used his experiences to write *Tales of the South Pacific* (1947). This was his first novel, published at age 40. The book won the Pulitzer Prize in 1948. It was made into a smash hit Broadway musical and film, both titled *South Pacific*.

Michener often commented during his life that he never considered himself a great writer. But he always felt that he could write better than a lot of the stuff he was reading. He believed that every young girl or young boy who aspired to a life as an artist was good enough to be successful, whether as a writer, an actor, or a musician. They were entitled, even obligated, to believe in themselves.

Michener believed that writers should follow their

own unique path, discover their own voice, develop their own model, and find out how they fit into the scheme of things. What others do might be interesting but not something to replicate.

During his life he sold an estimated 75 million copies of his more than 40 published books worldwide. His novels were translated into virtually every language in the world. He received five honorary doctorates from different universities and the nation's highest civilian award, the Medal of Freedom, in 1977.

Raised in poverty but with a full measure of love, James Michener lived his life with love for other people and their unique lives. Incorporating them into his stories made him a very rich man. At the time of his death at age 90, James Albert Michener had given away more than $100 million to charity.

John Keats

British Romantic Period Poet
(October 13, 1795 – February 23, 1821)

John Keats

Stop and consider! Life is but a day;
A fragile dew-drip on its perilous way *(p. 116)*

The noble heart that harbours virtuous thought,
And is with child of glorious great intent,
Can never rest until it forth have brought
Th' eternal brood of glory excellent *(p. 136)*

Taken from John Keats: his life and poetry, his friends, critics, and afterfame:
By Sir Sidney Colving. Macmillan and Co., Limited: London, 1920.

For many 21st century students, the study of poetry is not much fun but almost impossible to avoid completely. English classes require at least a basic knowledge. And teachers love to teach the very old poetry that often sounds like a different language.

Yet poetry is the spiritual core of every language ever spoken—Russian, Arabic, Chinese, Spanish, English, every language. Poetry embodies the best of human communication scrubbed down to its bare-rock essentials. Great poetry lives forever.

John Keats (1795–1821) is considered one of the greatest poets of the English Romantic Period. His poetry has had an increasing impact after his death, nearly 200 years ago, than when he lived.

As a 20-year-old man, Keats gave up a promising

career as a medical doctor to write poetry. During his life he published only three slim volumes of poetry. About 200 copies were sold prior to his death. Virtually all the major poetry critics ridiculed his writing. Some even suggested that he should do the world a favor— give up poetry and get a real job.

He died still a young man, at the age of 25, in such horrible pain that he hallucinated much of the time. His doctor refused to give him any pain medication (opium) for fear he would use it to commit suicide. In his last letter to his one true love, he told her that his life had been a complete and utter failure. A broken man, he requested that his gravestone be engraved with this sentence: "Here lies One Whose Name was writ in Water."

Yet, long after his death John Keats's legacy continued to grow until he became one of the great standard bearers of the Romantic Era in literature. Today, he is judged to be one of the greatest poets of the English language.

The Romantic Era (late 1700s to early 1800s), which included music, literature and poetry, evolved as a direct rebellion against the Age of Reason (or Enlightenment). The Age of Enlightenment (early to mid-1700s) was controlled by the brain. Anything that could be proven intellectually, scientifically, or mathematically ruled the day. The Romantic Era was influenced primarily by human emotion.

By most standards John Keats lived a normal middle-class childhood in London until the age of nine when his father was killed, fracturing his skull falling from a horse. This began the family's slide into poverty.

His mother remarried within weeks, but the marriage ended very soon. A few years later she began to show the first symptoms of tuberculosis, which was called consumption at that time. Much of John's early teens revolved around her worsening health. Her death in 1810 when he was 14 greatly affected the sensitive young man. The four orphaned children were left to the custody of their grandmother, who did not survive long after.

At the age of 16, John apprenticed with an apothecary (pharmacist) and three years later went on to become a medical student at Guys Hospital. He did so well that within a month he was appointed to a dressership, which meant he was a surgeon's assistant during operations. This indicated a distinct talent for medicine and his relatives began to believe that medicine would become his lifelong career, which would ensure his financial security.

In 1816 at the age of 20, he received his apothecary's license, which included a physician's and surgeon's license. Yet Keats's great love and the driving force of his life was poetry. According to his brother George, John "feared that he should never be a poet," even suggesting that it would destroy John if he could not achieve his dream. By the end of the year, Keats gave up his medical training and began his full-time career as a poet.

Within a few months John published his first book of poetry. The book received little interest from the public. Literary critics dismissed his poetry, labeling him a "pretender" to a poetic career. Even his publishers were ashamed of the book.

Released from the time constraints of practicing medicine and despite the poor reviews, Keats submerged himself into his poetry. He began to travel, including a four-month walking tour around the north of England, Scotland, and Ireland, delving deeply into his genius and focusing exclusively on poetry. However, he caught a bad cold that cut the trip short, and then he had to nurse his brother Tom, who died a few months later from tuberculosis.

Two events occurred, almost simultaneously, that changed his life. He met Francis "Fanny" Brawne, with whom he fell completely in love. He also began to feel the first stirrings of tuberculosis, the same illness that had killed his mother and his brother.

Much of his greatest writing came during this period. Inspired by his love for Fanny and obsessed by his conviction that death was rapidly approaching, the two combined to drive him forward in an outpouring of genius. He wrote of Fanny and death, "I have two luxuries to brood over in my walks, your loveliness, and the hour of my death." His love for Fanny was hopeless because his lack of income would not allow them to marry, and because he was increasingly ill, but they stayed true to one another nevertheless.

Knowing that his illness was dangerous for Fanny,

they saw one another only through the windows of the home they both lived in. Fanny and her mother rented one half, and John Keats and his friends rented the other half. Every day they wrote letters to each other.

In February 1820 he wrote in bitter despair and pain to Fanny, "I have left no immortal work behind me—nothing to make my friends proud of my memory—but I have lov'd the principle of beauty in all things, and if I had time I would have made myself remember'd." The final line of one of his most famous poems, Ode on a Grecian Urn, says, "'Beauty is truth, truth beauty,' —that is all ye know on earth, and all ye need to know."

As his illness reached a critical point, he left England in September 1820 for Rome, hoping that a warmer climate would improve his health. In Rome, John Keats continued to decline and died five months later.

Fanny mourned for six years, which meant that she wore formal mourning clothes and observed strict social rules. She eventually married 12 years after the death of John Keats and went on to have three children. She outlived him by 40 years.

His friends embellished the simple line he wanted on his gravestone, writing the following epitaph: "This Grave contains all that was Mortal of a Young English Poet Who on his Death Bed, in the Bitterness of his Heart at the Malicious Power of his Enemies, Desired these Words to be engraven on his Tomb Stone: Here lies One Whose Name was writ in Water. 24 February 1821"

John Keats proved to be a master poet despite his contemporary critics' low opinions. In triumph, his final book of poetry began to turn the tide even before his death. Many who had criticized him began to applaud the wonder and beauty of his work. Even his most vocal and harshest detractors confessed to being "somewhat impressed."

Algernon Charles Swinburne, writing about Keats in the 1880s for the *Encyclopedia Britannica*, praised Keats's Ode to a Nightingale as "one of the final masterpieces of human work in all time and for all ages." Today, there is hardly a school or university in the English-speaking world that does not view John Keats as one of the greatest poets of all time.

John Lennon

Founding Member of the Beatles
(October 9, 1940 - December 8, 1980)

John Lennon

The lyric was a blunt accusation leveled at both parents, whom he believed had so grievously failed him: one by giving birth to him, then giving him away; the other by walking out on him when he was a toddler. "Mother, you had me/ But I never had you....Father, you left me/ But I never left you.
(p. 650)

Taken from John Lennon: The Life by Phillip Norman. Published by Anchor Canada, a division of Random House Canada Limited; 2009.

Only one rock-and-roll band ever conquered the world completely—the Beatles. Even today, 50 years after they shattered the foundations of the music industry, their influence still works its magic in unlikely places.

The legend lives on. In the opening weeks of 2011, a new museum to honor the Beatles opened in Buenos Aires, Argentina. Rodolfo Vazquez—a man barely out of diapers when John Lennon formed his first band, the Quarrymen—supplied the 2,500 items of memorabilia, barely a third of his collection.

Beginning in the early 1960s, the Beatles crashed the music scene and began to set the music agenda, dominating all other bands for almost a decade. According to the Recording Industry Association of America, by 1985 they sold more than one billion records, worldwide.

Each member of the band—John Lennon, Paul McCartney, George Harrison, and Ringo Starr—contributed a unique style of life and musical talent. Fans continue to argue the contributions of their favorite band member. But John Lennon, founder and acknowledged leader, was widely considered the most controversial and complex.

Lennon was born near the beginning of World War II in Liverpool, England, on October 9, 1940, during some of the heaviest German bombing of Britain, to Julia and Alf Lennon. He was named John Winston Lennon, "John" for his paternal grandfather and "Winston" for Prime Minister Winston Churchill. Often during his earliest years, mother and son huddled together in makeshift bomb shelters as Germany dropped thousands of bombs on England's manufacturing cities.

A merchant seaman, Alf rarely returned home but continued to support the family financially. This ended in 1943, when he abandoned his wife and son completely. Alf reappeared near the end of the war but Julia had moved on with her life and was pregnant with another man's child. After sporadic visits Alf disappeared completely from his son's life by 1946.

Because of Julia's unsettled lifestyle, she gave John into the care of her sister Mimi and her husband, George Smith, who became strong parental figures for him. He lived with his aunt and uncle for the remainder of his childhood and adolescence.

Julia remained a part of his life, visiting often. She bought him his first guitar in 1956. His non-stop playing prompted his aunt to draw a firm distinction between playing for a hobby and making a living, which she believed could not be done with such music.

After primary school John attended Quarry Bank High School where he started his first band, The Quarrymen. John met Paul McCartney in the summer of 1957. Impressed by his ability to tune a guitar and his memory for lyrics, he invited him to join the band.

In July of 1958, after a visit with Aunt Mimi, John's mother was struck and killed by the car of a drunken, off-duty policeman. Devastated, John began a two-year cycle of heavy drinking and fighting. Julia's tragic death also cemented his friendship with Paul McCartney, who lost his mother to cancer two years earlier.

In the winter of 1958, Paul introduced John to George Harrison. John thought George—three years younger—was too young to join the band. Eventually he relented after Harrison made an impromptu audition for him on the upper deck of a bus.

With the addition of Paul McCartney and George Harrison the band renamed itself, "Johnny and The Moondogs" followed by "The Silver Beetles." Eventually, they shortened the name to "The Beatles" purposefully misspelling the word by placing an "a" in the name.

As the band progressed in its various musical identities, John's interest in school diminished. He was known by classmates as an easy-going guy and a comic who casually criticized and mimicked the teachers and other faculty. When he failed to pass the graduation tests at Quarry, Aunt Mimi stepped in to intervene.

Through her efforts and those of the headmaster, the Liverpool College of Art accepted Lennon as a student. Though he never settled down to the conformity of art school and never graduated, he did meet his first wife there, Cynthia Powell.

In 1960, The Beatles were invited to play at a club in Hamburg, Germany. By this time, they had added a friend of Lennon's named Stuart Sutcliff as the bassist, along with Pete Best on drums.

The band proved to be a hit. Unfortunately, Paul McCartney and Pete Best were deported for setting a small fire at a cinema near where they were staying. Then George Harrison was deported for being underage. A few days later Lennon's work permit was revoked and he left for England. Stuart Sutcliff decided to stay in Germany with his girlfriend and died soon after from a brain hemorrhage.

Despite their peculiar visit to Germany, they had established themselves as an up-and-coming band. In 1962, George Martin of EMI Records agreed to sign the band to a record contract but insisted that they replace Pete Best as drummer. Ringo Starr joined the group.

The Beatles released their first album on February 11, 1963. Also in 1963, Julian Lennon was born to John and Cynthia Lennon.

In the greatest turning point of his life John Lennon met Yoko Ono in November 1966. He recognized her as a kindred spirit and they became inseparable. A divorce was granted to John and Cynthia in November 1968. John and Yoko were married on March 20, 1969.

After Lennon met Ono the group never toured again. Yet they continued to produce music and gain fans. They released *Sergeant Pepper's Lonely Hearts Club Band* and began their own record label, Apple Records.

Increasingly, Lennon's energies transferred more and more to his relationship with Yoko Ono. He officially left the group in September 1969, although the band had begun to fall apart much earlier.

Lennon and Ono became enthusiastic peace activists. In many ways they became the figureheads of the counter-culture movement of the late '60s and early '70s. Lennon continued to produce music as a solo artist and with his new band, the Plastic Ono Band. His compositions—"Imagine," "Give Peace a Chance," and others—became anthems for generations.

Lennon and Ono continued to live in the United States. For several years during the early '70s John fought deportation and harassment by Nixon-era conservatives. In 1976, the courts ruled in his favor and he became a permanent resident in his beloved New York City.

On December 8, 1980, Lennon was shot and killed in front of his apartment building, the Dakota, in New York City. His assailant, Mark David Chapman, remains in prison to this day.

In some ways, John Lennon's legacy continues to grow. A 2002 BBC poll voted John Lennon number eight among the 100 Greatest Britons. *Rolling Stone* Magazine listed him as 38th on its list of "The Immortals" in 2004. The Beatles remain ranked at #1 among "The Greatest Artists of All Time."

Ella Fitzgerald

**American Jazz and Song Vocalist
Known as the First Lady of Song**
(April 25, 1917 – June 15, 1996)

Ella Fitzgerald

"It isn't where you came from, its where you're going that counts."

"Just don't give up trying to do what you really want to do. Where there is love and inspiration, I don't think you can go wrong."

"The only thing better than singing is more singing."

(http://www.ellafitzgerald.com/about/quotes.html)

Ella Fitzgerald was born with an immense talent. She possessed a singing voice so pure that even angels paused to listen. Throughout her life she worked tirelessly to improve her gift and she became known as the "First Lady of Song."

Still, she faced a number of potentially crippling disadvantages. Although the desire to perform filled her soul, she was painfully shy. Nor did she possess the glamour often required of performers. Her first professional job almost fell through because band members didn't like her looks. Above all else, her developmental years as a teenager could not be described as anything but catastrophic.

Ella Fitzgerald was born in Newport News, Virginia, on April 25, 1917. While Ella was still a baby, her mother's common-law marriage ended and they moved to Yonkers, New York. There her mother, Temperance, moved in with Joseph Da Silva. Ella's half-sister, Frances Da Silva, was born a few years later.

When Ella was 15, her mother died from injuries from a car accident. Devastated, Ella moved in with an aunt but could not cope with the loss. Her grades plummeted and she began to skip school.

Her life continued to spiral downward. Crime bosses took notice of her desperation and employed her in low-level crime-related jobs. She worked as a lookout for prostitutes, and she became a numbers runner for a Mafia gambling organization.

The authorities caught up with Ella and placed her in the Colored Orphan Asylum in the Bronx. Then they transferred her to the New York Training School for Girls in Hudson, New York, nothing more than a reformatory school. Eventually she escaped and lived as a homeless person in Depression-era New York.

In happier times, when her mother was alive, Ella wanted more than anything else to be a dancer, but she also loved listening to music, especially jazz. When her mother brought home a recording of singer Connee Boswell, Ella replayed the recording over and over, memorizing each word, every intonation of voice.

At 16 she finally got her big break. Ella was offered the opportunity to perform at one of the "amateur nights" at the Apollo Theater in Harlem, New York. The Apollo represented the ultimate test for black performing artists.

Ella had practiced her dance numbers to perfection. Yet immediately preceding her chance on stage, the Edwards Sisters performed a series of exceptional dance routines that brought down the house. Ella Fitzgerald decided to sing instead. She sang two of Connee Boswell's songs and captured the audience completely, winning the first prize of $25.

This was the first step in a career that would span 60 years. She began to enter other amateur contests. She returned to the Apollo Theater time and again.

Her vocal range spanned three octaves, more than most opera singers. She possessed a nearly perfect purity of tone and impeccable diction.

Ella Fitzgerald would eventually become the most famous female jazz vocalist in the world. Newspapers and magazines hailed her as a marvel. In addition to jazz, her repertoire spanned nearly the entire spectrum of music. Even her rendition of the nursery rhyme "A Tisket, A Tasket" drew rave reviews and opened new audiences.

Success did not come simply by stepping onto a stage. She worked long, grueling hours, practicing and performing. Throughout her life she maintained a touring and recording schedule that would cripple other professional artists. Eventually, she would record 200 albums and 2000 songs.

Nor did her life simply flow from success to success. As a black woman living in a deeply segregated country, she experienced uncounted acts of discrimination, many small but others significant.

Although one of the most famous singers in the country, Fitzgerald, along with a few other performers, was framed by the police in Texas on drug charges during a Jazz concert at the Philharmonic. Fitzgerald described the scene at the police station as almost surreal. She was astounded when, along with the humiliation, the police requested her autograph. No drugs were ever found.

In Hollywood, the famous and segregated nightclub, Mocambo, refused to schedule Fitzgerald, until Marilyn Monroe stepped forward to force a change. Monroe promised to sit at a front row table each night, with all her friends, if Ella Fitzgerald performed. The Mocambo booked Fitzgerald's act.

Fitzgerald's intense shyness made her long journeys from performance to performance an ordeal. Fellow musicians described her as a lonely girl who kept to herself. She seldom accepted invitations to step out with other performers. Fitzgerald would simply say, "I do better when I sing."

Ella Fitzgerald suffered severe health problems in later years. In 1986, nearing 70, she underwent quintuple coronary bypass. Her severe diabetes left her legally blind, and doctors amputated both legs below the knees in 1993. She died from complications of the disease in Beverly Hills, California, on June 15, 1996.

In Ella Fitzgerald's extraordinary life she accomplished more than she could have imagined as a young woman full of dreams. During her life she won

13 Grammy Awards. She sang at the inaugural gala for President John F. Kennedy. She was awarded the National Medal of Arts by Ronald Reagan. George H. W. Bush presented her with the Presidential Medal Of Freedom.

Edgar Allan Poe

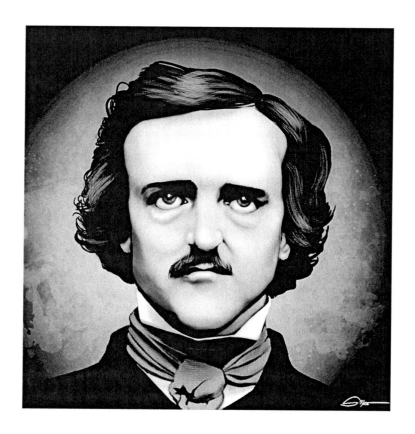

American Poet and Writer
of the Macabre
(January 19, 1809 – October 7, 1849)

Edgar Allan Poe

"It is a hard thing to be poor – but as I am kept so by an honest motive, I dare not complain." *(p. 183)*

"Even in the grave all is not lost. Else there is no immortality for man. Arousing from the most profound of slumbers, we break the gossamer web of some dream. Yet in a second afterwards (so frail may that web have been) we remember not that we have dreamed." *(p. 192)*

When first the said notes of my youthful lyre
Attracted thee unto my tuneful way-
That up life's rugged steep before me lay,
By fancy fashioned to my young desire,
And made alluring by Hope's beacon fire – *(p. 448)*

Taken from Edgar Allen Poe: his life, letters, and opinions by John Henry Ingram, Edgar Allen Poe. W.H. Allen and Co. London; 1886.

More than a century and half after his death, Edgar Allan Poe is still famous. He is not celebrated for some scientific step forward or for an agricultural success that helped to feed the world. He was not a legendary politician nor did he create great music.

He did, however, manage to look into the human soul and glimpse the darkness that lurks in the corners of the human mind. Somehow he managed to pull a small portion from the shadowy recesses into the light of day and put it on paper.

In his famous story "The Masque of the Red Death," Poe wrote of a country where plague called the "Red Death" was devastating the people. Prince Prospero gathers the wealthy and noble together and then he seals his palace doors. A great masquerade ball is held to rejoice in their victory over death. A man enters the dance wearing a "death mask." Enraged at the insult at such a joyous celebration, the Prince confronts the man. The mask is not a mask at all but the Red Death. The Red Death has penetrated the locked doors. The prince and all his guests die horribly.

Today bookshelves and bookstores overflow with tales of horror. Some of their authors enjoy fabulous wealth. Many consider Poe the father of the macabre (suggestive of the dance of death as the dictionary defines the term), because many of his stories have a grim or ghastly atmosphere. One would expect no less with such titles as: "The Masque of the Red Death," "The Imp of the Perverse," and "The Pit and the Pendulum."

Detective novels form an even larger part of the mystery genre. Most literary critics also credit Poe as the inventor of the modern crime story. Poe's story "The Murders in the Rue Morgue" certainly qualifies. It has the twists and turns for which Poe is famous. An orangutan is the prime murder suspect.

Romance is the most popular genre of writing today. As for romance, Poe's poem "Lenore" meets the requirements, as it contains the essential element of lost love. Unfortunately, the lady in question is dead and beginning to rot—Poe merged romance with the macabre.

Poe was not a novelist. He lived at a time when people looked to magazines and newspapers for their reading material. He crafted nearly all of his work for this market, mostly poetry and short stories. His only complete novel was *The Narrative of Arthur Gordon Pym*, a tale that verged on making Poe the father of modern science fiction, too.

Edgar Poe was born in Boston, Massachusetts, on January 19, 1809. His father abandoned the family sometime during the next year. His mother died of tuberculosis in the following year. John Allan, a successful merchant in Richmond, Virginia, took in the young boy and renamed him Edgar Allan Poe, although the family never formally adopted him.

In 1826, Poe became engaged to Sarah Royster. He also registered at the University of Virginia. He dropped out of college after one year, having become distanced from his foster father who refused to pay his gambling debts. Returning to Richmond, he discovered that Sarah was about to marry another man.

He traveled to Boston and attempted to support himself as a writer. When this endeavor failed, he joined the United States Army. Within two years he attained the rank of sergeant major, the highest noncommissioned rank available to him. After finding someone who would finish his enlisted term for him, he was discharged from the Army and entered the Military Academy at West Point in 1830.

A year later, entirely disenchanted with military life, Poe conceived a plan to force a dismissal from West Point. He deliberately neglected his military duties, such as participating in formation marching, attending classes and attending church. These breaches of conduct got him court-martialed in 1831 and the Academy dismissed him.

Poe never stopped writing during his time in the military. After his release from West Point, he published his third volume of poems, simply titled *Poems*. He financed the publication with small donations from his West Point friends.

Whatever the circumstances, Poe never lost his passion for writing. Although it was nearly impossible at that time, he tried to support himself by his writing. From poetry he switched his attention to short stories and began to publish in various small literary journals and magazines.

In 1835, at the age of 26, he secretly married his cousin Virginia Clemm. She was only 13 years old but was listed as 21 on the marriage certificate. His attempts to make a living from his writing alone were not successful. He worked off and on as an editor for various literary magazines, which also published his writings.

His wife, Virginia, began to show the first signs of tuberculosis in 1842, when she was barely 20 years of age. In response Poe began to drink more heavily, weighed down by the stress. Still, he continued to edit and publish poetry and stories.

On January 29, 1845, he published the narrative poem "The Raven," for which he received only nine dollars. The poem made him famous.

Poe moved into a small cottage in Brooklyn, New York. There, in what is known today as "Poe Cottage," Virginia died on January 30, 1847, at the age of 24.

Poe's behavior grew increasingly erratic after his wife's death. He began to seek out other women. An engagement to the poet Sarah Helen Whitman failed because of his drinking and instability. He returned to Richmond and attempted to resume his relationship with his childhood sweetheart, Sarah Royster, who was a widow at that time.

On October 3, 1849, Poe was found wandering the streets of Baltimore in a feverish state. He was taken to a hospital where he died a few days later. The cause of death still remains a mystery but newspapers of the time printed the meaningless medical catchphrase "congestion of the brain."

An anonymous article appeared in the *New York Tribune* after Poe's burial. In an article titled "Memoir of the Author," Poe was depicted as a depraved drunk and drug-addled madman. These lies were accepted in part because this article was the only biography available. It contained letters supposed to have been written by Poe. It was eventually attributed to Rufus Griswold, a man who hated Poe.

Over the years Griswold's fabrications were

disproved. The letters supposedly written by Edgar Allan Poe were revealed as forgeries. Poe was never a drug addict. He was, however, addicted to alcohol and probably depressed for much of his life.

Even today, Poe's stories and poems continue to make people shiver delightfully. He was the master and creator of his genre more than 160 years ago. He remains the undisputed father of the macabre.

Bertrand Russell

British Philosopher, Mathematician, Historian and Social Critic
(May 18, 1872 – February 2, 1970)

Bertrand Arthur William Russell

"I remember a very definite change when I reached what in modern child psychology is called 'latency period'. At this stage, I began to enjoy using slang, pretending to have no feelings, and being generally 'manly'. I began to despise my people, chiefly because of their extreme horror of slang and their absurd notion that it was dangerous to climb trees. So many things were forbidden me that I acquired the habit of deceit, in which I persisted up to the age of twenty-one." *(p. 33)*

"Socially I was shy, childish, awkward, well behaved, and good-natured. I used to watch with envy people who could manage social intercourse without anguished awkwardness." *(p. 36)*

"We are driven to conclude that the greatest mistake in human history was the discovery of truth. It has not made us free, except from delusions that comforted us, and restraints that preserved us; it has not made us happy, for truth is not beautiful, and did not deserve to be so passionately chased. As we look upon it now we wonder why we hurried so to find it." *(p. 444)*

Taken from The Autobiography of Bertrand Russell: by Bertrand Russell. Routledge, London; 1998.

The twentieth century produced few minds to equal the intensity of Bertrand Russell. Indeed, he stands among the greatest thinkers in history. Yet, he often stood directly in opposition to the established thinking of his day.

Great minds think outside the box and therefore push forward the boundaries of human thought. Yet, they often live their lives in ways not wholly accepted by their society. Russell fit this mold like few others of his time.

Russell became the standard bearer and intellectual prophet for tens of millions because of his lectures and writings on liberal philosophy and individual freedom. He would enrage millions more for the same thing.

Many people thought him a socialist, if not a communist. In fact, he openly applauded the people's revolution in Russia until he visited Moscow and interviewed Lenin. Russell came away deeply disillusioned and repelled by the brutality of Russian communism.

A public outcry in 1940 influenced the City College of New York to cancel his professorial appointment because he was "morally unfit." This action was confirmed by a court order. Eminent physicist Albert Einstein came to his defense, labeling his opponents as "mediocre minds."

He was passionately anti-war. During World War I, Trinity College dismissed him from their faculty and the British government imprisoned him for his activism against the war. Yet, in World War II, he encouraged any means necessary to destroy Hitler for the sake of humanity, pointing out that sometimes war was the lesser of two evils.

After the Second World War, he advocated that the Western powers should stop Stalin before the Soviet Union built their first nuclear weapon. At the height of the Cold War in 1955, Russell and Einstein together became prominent proponents of nuclear disarmament.

In the 1960s, Russell condemned the United States for its policies in Southeast Asia, especially the war in Vietnam. He became the icon for an entire generation of war protesters.

Bertrand Russell was born on May 18, 1872, at Ravenscroft, Wales, into the bluest of blue-blood aristocracy, an ancient and noble British family. His great-grandfather was the Duke of Bedford. His grandfather held the title of the 1st Earl Russell and twice served Queen Victoria as Prime Minister.

Bertrand's parents were both radically liberal in their thinking and behavior. His mother died of diphtheria just after Bertrand's second birthday. His father, John Russell (Viscount Amberley), was an avowed atheist. He died of bronchitis when Bertrand was three years old.

Bertrand and his brother went to live with their grandparents, the Earl and Countess Russell. At first Bertrand became entranced by Christianity and religious dogma, as well as by mathematics. But by the age of 18, he rejected all religion. He became the atheist his father had wanted.

Bertrand spent much of his young life feeling isolated. Unable to find anyone with whom to share his thoughts, he considered suicide, but his insatiable appetite for knowledge saved him. He couldn't end his life until he had learned more mathematics. He credited mathematics for keeping him alive.

He continued with mathematics, winning a scholarship to Cambridge University's Trinity College. After graduating with honors, he continued his studies, discovering "Russell's paradox" in 1901. It was a leap of genius understood by few outside the world of mathematics.

His book, *Principles of Mathematics*, written before he was 30 and published in 1903, put him on the world stage. He followed this in 1910, 1912, and 1913 with a three-volume set, *Principia Mathematica*, written with Alfred North Whitehead, a famous English mathematician. Russell became world famous among mathematicians.

If Bertrand Russell had limited himself to the narrow world of mathematics, he would have been remembered as a genius only by those who could understand his work. Yet, he could not avoid his progressive roots. Even his staunch Victorian grandmother believed in Darwinism and supported Irish Home Rule, both radical ideas for her time.

At the same time that Russell excelled in mathematics, he studied and wrote on philosophy. As he matured, he immersed himself in the study of logic, metaphysics, the philosophy of language, and epistemology (the nature and limits of human knowledge).

He wrote on nearly every aspect of philosophy except aesthetics (beauty and human emotions toward beauty). When asked why he excluded aesthetics, he replied that he did not know anything about aesthetics, although, he joked, he frequently seemed to write on subjects about which he knew nothing.

Russell possessed an astounding capacity to express his thoughts in ways any intelligent person could understand. It was this clarity that brought him worldwide attention.

His views were easy to understand. He urged people not to be deterred from gaining an education by people who made the pursuit seem either too easy or too hard. He protested against the social status quo that allowed the stronger to bully the weaker members of society. He said that the main trouble with the world was that ignorant people with confidence were the leaders, while intelligent people with doubts were not. His view of capitalism was that its advocates appealed to liberty to preserve their system in which those who made all the money could keep abusing those who did not. Cooperation, he thought, was the key to improving all of humankind.

Bertrand Russell continued to express his thoughts to the very end. He published his three-volume autobiography in 1967, 1968, and 1969. He died at the age of 97 on February 2, 1970.

Malcolm X

Muslim Minister and Human Rights Activist
(May 19, 1925 – February 21, 1965)

Malcolm X
El-Hajj Malik El-Shabazz

"The hardest test I ever faced in my life was praying. You understand... bending my knees to pray – that act – well, that took me a week.

"You know what my life had been. Picking a lock to rob someone's house was the only way my knees had ever been bent before.

"I had to force myself to bend my knees. And waves of shame and embarrassment would force me back up."
(pp. 169-170)

"One day, I remember, a dirty glass of water was on a counter and Mr. Muhammad put a clean glass of water beside it. "You want to know how to spread my teachings?" he said, and he pointed to the glass of water. "Don't' condemn if you see a person has a dirty glass of water," he said, "just show them the clean glass of water that you have. When they inspect it, you won't have to say that yours is better." *(p. 205)*

Taken from The Autobiography of Malcolm X. Written by Malcolm X with the assistance of Alex Haley. Ballantine Books, New York; 1973.

The hero of this story never won the grand prize. He struggled, as everyone expects all heroes to struggle. He gave his best efforts, typical of a hero. He overcame great obstacles, but he was murdered before the story was complete.

Malcolm X lived a life of controversy. He took a

hard line that allowed little room for compromise. He made a lot of people nervous.

Yet, he was and remains a champion for many—a black man in ebony armor on a sable stallion.

He grew up in a time of stark racism, when the economic, social, and political separation of blacks and whites remained almost absolute. The dream of civil rights in America—equal opportunity and personal liberty—glimmered but faintly in the distant future.

A dynamic speaker, he preached black supremacy. In the first part of his life, he encouraged the separation of white and black Americans. This echoed in the hearts of some. For others, his message conflicted too sharply with the emphasis on integration advocated by other black civil rights leaders.

Yet, Malcolm X proved himself capable of personal evolution. Shortly before his death he reached a critical crossroads in his life and philosophy. He attained an epiphany, a clarity of insight. After his pilgrimage to Mecca, he disavowed racism. He declared his desire to work with other civil rights leaders to achieve a permanent change in society. In Mecca he met men he could call brothers who were light skinned, with blue eyes and blonde hair.

Malcolm Little was born on May 19, 1925, in Omaha, Nebraska. His mother, Louise, worked in the home caring for Malcolm and his seven brothers and sisters. His father, Earl, a Baptist minister, held fast to the teachings of Marcus Garvey, a Jamaican activist who espoused the Back-to-Africa movement.

Receiving death threats from white supremacists, Earl moved the family twice before Malcolm was four years old. Still, their home in Lansing, Michigan, was burned to the ground in 1929. Two years later Malcolm's father was struck by a streetcar and killed.

The police reports concluded that both instances were accidents. The black community believed otherwise. The insurance companies refused to pay all of the insurance policies, claiming that Earl had committed suicide.

By the time Malcolm reached his eighth birthday his mother suffered a nervous breakdown and was committed to an institution. The state split the family and placed the children in different foster homes.

Malcolm was an extraordinary student. In junior high he graduated first in his class. Yet, when he confided his career goal to become a lawyer to a favorite teacher, he received a cruel surprise. Using the most brutal language possible, the teacher told him that someone with his skin color could never reach his goal. Malcolm dropped out of school in eighth grade concluding that the white world would not allow a black man to succeed.

Malcolm moved to Boston where he worked low-paying jobs. Wanting more from life, he moved to Harlem, New York, and took up the life of a smalltime criminal. He became deeply involved in narcotics, prostitution, and gambling.

Back in Boston, Malcolm was arrested in 1946 and sentenced to ten years in prison for burglary. Throughout his incarceration he received visits from his brother Reginald, who had become a Muslim and joined a religious organization called the Nation of Islam.

Malcolm received parole after seven years. He emerged from prison a Muslim, like his brother, and a fervent believer in Elijah Mohammed, the leader of the Nation of Islam. In prison he renamed himself, dropping the surname "Little" as a slave name. He replaced it with "X" to denote his tribal name, lost when his ancestors were brought to America in chains.

He devoted himself to the Nation of Islam. Quickly his natural charisma and intelligence became evident, and Elijah Mohammed selected Malcolm as the national spokesman. People flocked to his message and the Nation of Islam grew from 500 in 1952 to 30,000 in 1963.

At the high point of the civil rights movement in 1963, Malcolm experienced a crisis of faith. He learned that the man he admired above all others, Elijah Mohammed, was corrupt.

The information devastated Malcolm, a true believer. He refused to participate in a cover-up for a man he had once considered a living prophet. He terminated his relationship with the Nation of Islam in 1964, and founded the Muslim Mosque, Inc.

After his separation from the Nation of Islam

he made a pilgrimage (traditional Muslim Hajj) to Mecca, Saudi Arabia. The journey changed his life. He returned with a renewed hope for the future and a new vision for the integration of black and white America.

Within a year after his return from Mecca, he was targeted for assassination. His home was firebombed on February 14, 1965. Miraculously his family escaped injury.

A week later, on February 21, 1965, he was scheduled to speak in Manhattan at the Audubon Ballroom. Three gunmen, all members of the Nation of Islam, rushed onto the stage and shot him 15 times. He was pronounced dead at New York's Columbia Presbyterian Hospital. He was only 39 years old. Months later his wife, Betty, gave birth to their twin daughters.

A few years before his death, Malcolm had changed his name to El-Hajj Malik El-Shabazz. His wife, Betty Shabazz, received condolences from around the world, including from Martin Luther King Jr., who expressed sorrow over "the shocking and tragic assassination of your husband."

Malcolm X left a legacy that is remembered even today. His autobiography has remained a favorite among students. He has been the subject of a number of books and movies. In 1992, Denzel Washington received an Oscar nomination for his performance as the title character in Spike Lee's critically acclaimed movie, *Malcolm X*.

George Washington Carver

American Agriculturalist and Inventor
(January 1864 – January 5, 1943)

George Washington Carver

"No individual has any right to come into the world and go out of it without leaving behind him distinct and legitimate reasons for having passed through it." *George Washington Carver, May 25, 1915.*

Taken From George Washington Carver: In His Own Words. By George Washington Carver, Gary K Kremer. 1987, University of Missouri Press, Columbia Missouri.

"Fear of something is at the root of hate for others and hate within will eventually destroy the hater. Keep your thoughts free from hate, and you need have no fear from those who hate you…"

Taken from George Washing Carver, scientists and symbol – Linda O McMurry, pg. 107. Oxford University Press, Oxford, 1981.

Of all the statements below only one is incorrect. Take this quick quiz and pick which statement about George Washington Carver is not true:

- Born a slave.
- Kidnapped by marauders as a baby with his mother. His mother was never found.
- Left home at ten years old, walking from town to town to gain an education.
- Accepted at college but turned away when they discovered he was black.

- Earned a Master's Degree and became the first black professor at Iowa State Agricultural College.
- Became a concert pianist and artist of international reputation.
- Saved the Southern economy from ruin.
- Invented peanut butter.

Nearly all the biographies, essays and articles about George Washington Carver credit him as the inventor of that unequaled lunchbox ingredient—peanut butter. They are all wrong. George never invented peanut butter.

However, it is true that Professor Carver possessed a remarkable talent for agricultural invention. Early in the 20th century he invented over 100 new ways to utilize sweet potatoes, soybeans, and pecans. From the lowly peanut (called "goober peas" in the South) he concocted almost 300 original products. He even created commercial clothing dyes from the very soils of Alabama.

Peanut butter, however, did not originate with Professor Carver.

The secret process for peanut butter consists of nothing more than mashing peanuts into a paste. Every culture that consumed peanuts produced peanut butter, even the Aztecs and the Mayans. It is almost a certainty, however, that George Washington Carver produced peanut butter for his own enjoyment and he probably put it on bread for lunch.

Among his most notable triumphs, he developed a method to resurrect Southern agriculture, the financial lifeblood of the South. During a time when cotton and tobacco had nearly destroyed the soil, George developed a system of crop rotation that won the day. It was a simple thing, but powerful. Ironically, a black man, a former slave, saved the South.

George was born a slave toward the end of the Civil War, probably in 1864 or 1865, in the far west state of Missouri. His mother was owned by a German-American immigrant named Moses Carver. His father was thought to be a slave on a neighboring farm who died in a logging accident before George's birth.

During the Civil War, Missouri suffered from nearly endless waves of marauders and gangs of thieves. Some rode under flags from both the North and the South. Others were renegades and used the state as their personal piggy bank. When George was only a few days old, night raiders attacked the Carver farm and stole George's mother and him. George's mother was never found.

With the abolition of slavery, Moses Carver and his wife, Susan, decided to raise George and his brother James as their own children. George remembered his adoptive parents as kind people. His foster mother taught him to read and write at a young age. This opened the floodgates to his imagination and inflamed a lifelong passion for education.

At the age of ten, as a black child, he was rejected

from attending the local school. He walked to a neighboring town to attend elementary school. As the need arose he continued to move, seeking greater educational opportunities.

George eventually gained admission to Highland College. Unfortunately, when he arrived, the school's president revoked George's admission because the school, he said, did not take "Negroes."

Still, George's hunger for knowledge continued to drive him forward. Simpson College accepted his application in 1887. They offered no science classes, so he studied art and piano and became an expert pianist and artist. The World's Columbian Exhibition of 1893, held in Chicago, displayed one of his paintings.

Later, he transferred to Iowa State Agricultural College to study botany, his first love. Upon graduation he joined the faculty as the first black professor and earned a Master of Agriculture Degree.

In 1896, at the age of 36, his life took a dramatic change. Booker T. Washington, a powerful spokesman for the Black community, visited George and offered him a teaching position at his new college in Tuskegee, Alabama. George accepted the position and remained there for 47 years.

If the story ended at this point, it would provide evidence of an exceptional man who beat impossible odds and achieved his dreams through nothing more than intelligence and determination. But this was just the beginning.

An economic crisis finally established George's

scientific genius. For decades there were only two Southern cash crops, cotton and tobacco. With the soil exhausted and harvests falling below the financial break-even point, a financial disaster for the entire South appeared inevitable.

Professor Carver developed a crop rotation system to restore nitrogen to the soil using peanuts, cow peas, and sweet potatoes. In the farmers' eyes the results were almost magical. Both cotton and tobacco rebounded.

But praise for Carver's efforts lasted only a few years. While farmers rejoiced to see abundant cotton crops resulting from the reinvigorated soil, their barns were filling with peanuts and sweet potatoes, with nearly no market for them.

Professor Carver went to work to produce saleable products to help farmers empty their bursting storehouses. He developed over 300 products from the lowly peanut, including milk, cheese, soap, shampoo, ink, facial cream, and massage oil.

It was this endeavor that earned Carver a worldwide reputation as a master agricultural inventor. Thomas Edison, the famous inventor, was so impressed that he offered him a job at $100,000 a year (nearly one million dollars in today's economy). Carver decided to stay at Tuskegee. Around this same time, another famous inventor, Henry Ford, became impressed with Carver's work and contacted him, which led to the two men becoming lifelong friends.

Carver could have become very wealthy. Despite

his vast number of inventions and innovations, he applied for only three U.S. patents during his life. When asked why he refused to patent most of his discoveries, he responded, "God gave them to me, how can I sell them to someone else?" For him money was never the primary object of his desire.

George Washington Carver was born a slave. He died as one of America's greatest scientists, on January 5, 1943, at the age of 78.

The motto for his life could be summed up in his own words. "When you do the common things in life in an uncommon way, you will command the attention of the world."

Research Methodology

Most of us readily accept the Internet as an entertainment highway. We are less confident about its power to educate—to provide us with accurate information. Therein rests the challenge. Whom to trust? Uncertainty is a constant companion.

Of course, the Internet has greatly assisted the efforts of scholars to reveal historical truths. The digitization of historical records saves researchers endless months and even years. Search engines may never completely eliminate digging through the rare collections and backroom vaults of America's impressive libraries, but they help.

Our task was much different from the challenges faced by learned academics. The lives and public personae of the celebrated individuals in this book are well known. The historical details are readily available online and accessible to anyone, world wide.

We simply gathered and collated the information from as many available sources as practical.

We invite the young reader to go online and explore.

Resources

Maya Angelou
- Maya Angelou: Global Renaissance Woman. Official Website. http:// mayaangelou.com/ Accessed on September 13, 2011
- Maya Angelou. Academy of Achievement. http://www.achievement. org/autodoc/page/ang0int-1 Accessed on September 13, 2011
- Maya Angelou. Poets.org. http://www.poets.org/poet.php/ prmPID/87 Accessed on September 13, 2011
- Maya Angelou. Wikipedia. http://en.wikipedia.org/wiki/Maya_ Angelou Accessed on September 13, 2011
- Maya Angelou Biography. Biography.com. http://www.biography. com/articles/Maya-Angelou-9185388 Accessed on September 13, 2011
- Maya Angelou Quotes. Goodreads.org. http://www.goodreads.com/ author/quotes/3503.Maya_Angelou Accessed on September 13, 2011

Aristotle
- Aristotle. Internet Encyclopedia of Philosophy. http://www.iep.utm. edu/aristotl/ Accessed on September 18, 2011
- Aristotle. Shields, Christopher, "Aristotle," The Stanford Encyclopedia of Philosophy (Spring 2012 Edition), Edward N. Zalta (ed.), http://plato.stanford.edu/archives/spr2012/entries/aristotle/ Accessed on March 15, 2012
- Aristotle. University of California Museum of Paleontology. http://www.ucmp.berkeley.edu/history/aristotle.html Accessed on September 18, 2011
- Aristotle. Wikipedia. http://en.wikipedia.org/wiki/Aristotle Accessed on September 18, 2011
- Aristotle Quotes. BrainyQuote. http://www.brainyquote.com/ quotes/authors/a/aristotle.html Accessed on September 18, 2011

Louis Armstrong
- Louis "Satchmo" Armstrong. http://www.redhotjazz.com/louie.html Accessed on February 15, 2011
- Louis Armstrong. SwingMusic.Net. http://www.swingmusic.net/ ArmstrongLouis.html Accessed on February 15, 2011
- Louis Armstrong. Wikipedia. http://en.wikipedia.org/wiki/Louis_ Armstrong Accessed on February 15, 2011
- Louis Armstrong Biography. http://www.biography.com/articles/

Louis-Armstrong-9188912 Accessed on February 15, 2011
- Louis Armstrong Biography. http://www.essortment.com/louis-armstrong-biography-20468.html Accessed on February 15, 2011

Johann Sebastian Bach
- Johann Sebastian Bach. Aaron Green. About.com. Johann Sebastian Bach. http://classicalmusic.about.com/od/classicalcomposers/p/bach.htm Accessed on February 01, 2011
- Johann Sebastian Bach. Answers.com. http://www.answers.com/topic/johann-sebastian-bach Accessed on February 01, 2011
- Johann Sebastian Bach: Baroque Composer. EnchantedLearning.com. http://www.enchantedlearning.com/music/bios/bach/ Accessed on February 01, 2011
- Johann Sebastian Bach. BaroqueMusic.org. http://www.baroquemusic.org/bqxjsbach.html Accessed on February 01, 2011
- Johann Sebastian Bach. Wikipedia. http://en.wikipedia.org/wiki/Johann_Sebastian_Bach Accessed on February 01, 2011

Ingrid Bergman
- Ingrid Bergman. New York Times. http://movies.nytimes.com/person/5652/Ingrid-Bergman/biography Accessed on February 10, 2011
- Ingrid Bergman. NNDB. http://www.nndb.com/people/836/000024764/ Accessed on February 10, 2011
- Ingrid Berman. Turner Classic Movies. http://www.tcm.com/tcmdb/participant.jsp?participantId=14558|72764 Accessed on February 10, 2011
- Ingrid Bergman. Wikipedia. http://en.wikipedia.org/wiki/Ingrid_Bergman Accessed on February 10, 2011
- Ingrid Bergman Biography. http://www.ingridbergman.com/about/bio.htm Accessed on February 10, 2011

George Washington Carver
- George Washington Carver. About.com. http://inventors.about.com/od/cstartinventors/a/GWC.htm Accessed on February 20, 2011
- George Washington Carver. Gale Cengage Learning. http://www.gale.cengage.com/free_resources/bhm/bio/carver_g.htm Accessed on February 20, 2011
- George Washington Carver. http://www.ideafinder.com/history/inventors/carver.htm Accessed on February 20, 2011
- George Washington Carver. http://www.africawithin.com/bios/george_carver.htm Accessed on February 20, 2011
- George Washington Carver. Wikipedia. http://en.wikipedia.org/wiki/George_Washington_Carver Accessed on February 20, 2011
- George Washington Carver Quotes. Wikiquote. http://en.wikiquote.org/wiki/George_Washington_Carver Accessed on February 20, 2011

Bill Clinton

- Bill Clinton 1993-2001. The White House. http://www.whitehouse.gov/about/presidents/williamjclinton Accessed on October 30, 2011
- Bill Clinton. Wikipedia. http://en.wikipedia.org/wiki/Bill_Clinton Accessed on October 30, 2011
- Bill Clinton Foundation. William J. Clinton Foundation. http://www.clintonfoundation.org/ Accessed on October 30, 2011
- Bill Clinton Library. William J. Clinton Presidential Library. http://www.clintonlibrary.gov/ Accessed on October 30, 2011
- Bill Clinton Quotes. Wikiquote. http://en.wikiquote.org/wiki/Bill_Clinton Accessed on October 30, 2011

Frederick Douglass

- Frederick Douglass. Merriman, C.D., for Jalic Inc. The Literature Network, 2008. http://www.online-literature.com/frederick_douglass/ Accessed on January 15, 2011
- Frederick Douglass, "My Experience and Mission to Great Britain." The Gilder Lehrman Center for the Study of Slavery, Resistance & Abolition. The MacMillan Center, Yale University. http://www.yale.edu/glc/archive/1059.htm Accessed on January 15, 2011
- Frederick Douglas. Western New York Suffragists, Rochester Regional Library Council, 2000. http://www.winningthevote.org/FDouglass.html Accessed on January 15, 2011
- Frederick Douglass. Wikipedia. http://en.wikipedia.org/wiki/Frederick_Douglass Accessed on January 15, 2011

Ella Fitzgerald

- Ella Fitzgerald. Hanna Wong. First Lady of Song. Library of Congress. http://www.loc.gov/loc/lcib/9708/ella.html Accessed on October 26, 2011
- Ella Fitzgerald. The Official Site of the First Lady of Song. http://www.ellafitzgerald.com/ Accessed on October 26, 2011
- Ella Fitzgerald, Something to Live For. PBS American Masters. http://www.pbs.org/wnet/americanmasters/episodes/ella-fitzgerald/something-to-live-for/590/ Accessed on October 26, 2011
- Ella Fitzgerald. Wikipedia. http://en.wikipedia.org/wiki/Ella_Fitzgerald Accessed on October 26, 2011
- Ella Fitzgerald Quotes. Brainy Quote. http://www.brainyquote.com/quotes/authors/e/ella_fitzgerald.html Accessed on October 26, 2011

Alexander Hamilton

- Alexander Hamilton. http://www.law.umkc.edu/faculty/projects/ftrials/burr/hamiltonbio.htm Accessed on February 03, 2011
- Alexander Hamilton. Ian Finseth. "The Rise and Fall of Alexander Hamilton." http://xroads.virginia.edu/~cap/ham/hamilton.html Accessed on February 03, 2011
- Alexander Hamilton. Wikipedia. http://en.wikipedia.org/wiki/

Alexander_Hamilton Accessed on February 03, 2011
- Alexander Hamilton Biography. http://www.biography.com/articles/ Alexander-Hamilton-9326481 Accessed on February 03, 2011
- Alexander Hamilton Quotes. Wikiquote. http://en.wikiquote.org/ wiki/Alexander_Hamilton Accessed on February 03, 2011

Joseph Haydn
- Franz Joseph Haydn. Aaron Green. About.com. http:// classicalmusic.about.com/od/classicalcomposers/p/haydnprofile. htm Accessed on October 24, 2011
- Franz Joseph Haydn. Kevin Knight. New Advent. http://www. newadvent.org/cathen/07158b.htm Accessed on October 24, 2011
- Joseph Haydn. Oracle ThinkQuest. http://library.thinkquest. org/22673/haydn.html Accessed on October 24, 2011
- Joseph Haydn. Wikipedia. http://en.wikipedia.org/wiki/Joseph_ Haydn Accessed on October 24, 2011
- Joseph Haydn Quotes. Wikiquote. http://en.wikiquote.org/wiki/ Joseph_Haydn Accessed on October 24, 2011

Stonewall Jackson
- Stonewall Jackson. Wikipedia. http://en.wikipedia.org/wiki/ Stonewall_Jackson Accessed on October 26, 2011
- Stonewall Jackson Quotes. Wikiquote. http://en.wikiquote.org/wiki/ Stonewall_Jackson Accessed on October 26, 2011
- Stonewall Jackson Resources. Virginia Military Institute. http://www. vmi.edu/archives.aspx?id=3747 Accessed on October 26, 2011
- Thomas Jonathan Jackson. Stewart Sifakis. Shotgun's Home of the American Civil War. http://www.civilwarhome.com/jackbio.htm Accessed on October 26, 2011
- Thomas Jonathan "Stonewall" Jackson. University of Virginia. http://xroads.virginia.edu/~ug97/monument/jacksbio.html Accessed on October 26, 2011

Steve Jobs
- Steve Jobs. allaboutSteveJobs.com. http://allaboutstevejobs.com/ Accessed on October 26, 2011
- Steve Jobs. Bio. http://www.biography.com/people/steve-jobs-9354805 Accessed on October 26, 2011
- Steve Jobs. "How to live before you die." TED: Ideas Worth Spreading. http://www.ted.com/talks/steve_jobs_how_to_live_ before_you_die.html Accessed on October 26, 2011
- Steve Jobs. Apple Website. "Remembering Steve." http://www.apple. com/stevejobs/ Accessed on October 26, 2011
- Steve Jobs. Wikipedia. http://en.wikipedia.org/wiki/Steve_Jobs Accessed on October 26, 2011
- Steve Paul Jobs. Lee Angetelli. Virginia Tech. http://ei.cs. vt.edu/~history/Jobs.html Accessed on October 26, 2011

- Steve Jobs Quotes. The Best Steve Jobs Quotes From His Biography. Business Insider. http://www.businessinsider.com/best-steve-jobs-quotes-from-biography-2011-10 Accessed on October 26, 2011

Benito Juárez
- Benito Juárez. Casey Carr. East Side Union High School District. http://staff.esuhsd.org/balochie/studentprojects/benitojuarez/index.html October 26, 2011
- Benito Juárez. Jim Tuck. "Mexico's Lincoln: The ecstasy and agony of Benito Juárez." Mexconnect. http://www.mexconnect.com/articles/274-mexico-s-lincoln-the-ecstasy-and-agony-of-benito-juarez October 26, 2011
- Benito Juárez: Mexico's Liberal Reformer. About.com. http://latinamericanhistory.about.com/od/19thcenturylatinamerica/p/benitojuarez.htm Accessed on October 26, 2011
- Benito Juárez. NNDB. http://www.nndb.com/people/945/000091672/ Accessed on October 26, 2011
- Benito Juárez. Wikipedia. http://en.wikipedia.org/wiki/Benito_JuC3A1rez Accessed on October 26, 2011
- Benito Juárez Quotes. Wikiquote. http://en.wikiquote.org/wiki/Benito_JuC3A1rez Accessed on October 26, 2011

John Keats
- John Keats. http://academic.brooklyn.cuny.edu/english/melani/cs6/keats.html Accessed on February 02, 2011
- John Keats. The Life and Work of John Keats. http://englishhistory.net/keats.html Accessed on February 02, 2011
- John Keats. The Literature Network. http://www.online-literature.com/keats/ Accessed on February 02, 2011
- John Keats. Poets.org. http://www.poets.org/poet.php/prmPID/66 Accessed on February 02, 2011
- John Keats. Wikipedia. http://en.wikipedia.org/wiki/John_Keats Accessed on February 02, 2011

Rudyard Kipling
- Rudyard Kipling. "Something of Myself" in public domain. 03/14/2012 http://www.telelib.com/authors/K/KiplingRudyard/prose/SomethingOfMyself/index.html Accessed on February 16, 2011
- Rudyard Kipling. Answers.com http://www.answers.com/topic/rudyard-kipling Accessed on February 16, 2011
- Rudyard Kipling. http://www.readprint.com/author-54/Rudyard-Kipling-books#anchor_biography Accessed on February 16, 2011
- Rudyard Kipling. Wikipedia. http://en.wikipedia.org/wiki/Rudyard_Kipling Accessed on February 14, 2011
- Rudyard Kipling Biography. Nobelprize.org. 18 Feb 2011 http://nobelprize.org/nobel_prizes/literature/laureates/1907/kipling-bio.

html Accessed on February 16, 2011

John Lennon

- John Lennon. Official website. http://www.johnlennon.com/ Accessed on February 25, 2011
- John Lennon. Wikipedia. http://en.wikipedia.org/wiki/John_Lennon Accessed on February 25, 2011
- John Lennon Biography. http://www.biography.com/people/john-lennon-9379045 Accessed on March 15, 2012
- John Lennon FBI Files. http://www.lennonfbifiles.com/ Accessed on February 25, 2011

Art Linkletter

- Art Linkletter. "Art Linkletter: He Says the Darndest Things About His Life and New Quest." The Wall Street Journal March 11, 2009. http://online.wsj.com/article/SB123673035387989403.html Accessed on September 18, 2011
- Art Linkletter. "Art Linkletter, TV Host, Dies at 97." New York Times. May 26, 2010. http://www.nytimes.com/2010/05/27/arts/27linkletter.html Accessed on September 18, 2011
- Art Linkletter. Wikipedia. http://en.wikipedia.org/wiki/Art_Linkletter Accessed on September 18, 2011
- Art Linkletter Biography. Biography.com. http://www.biography.com/articles/Art-Linkletter-9542345 Accessed on September 18, 2011
- Art Linkletter Interview with Gary James. FamousInterview.com http://www.famousinterview.ca/interviews/art_linkletter.htm Accessed on September 18, 2011
- Art Linkletter Quotes. Brainy Quotes. http://www.brainyquote.com/quotes/authors/a/art_linkletter.html Accessed on September 18, 2011

James A. Michener

- James A. Michener. Academy of Achievement. http://www.achievement.org/autodoc/page/mic0int-1 Accessed on February 04, 2011
- James A. Michener. Answers.com. http://www.answers.com/topic/james-a-michener Accessed on February 04, 2011
- James A. Michener. Kira Albin. "Interview: James Michener An Epic Life." http://www.grandtimes.com/michener.html Accessed on February 04, 2011
- James A. Michener. Wikipedia. http://en.wikipedia.org/wiki/James_A._Michener Accessed on February 04, 2011
- James A. Michener Quotes. Brainy Quote. http://www.brainyquote.com/quotes/authors/j/james_a_michener.html Accessed on February 04, 2011

Marilyn Monroe

- Marilyn Monroe. Answers.com. http://www.answers.com/topic/ marilyn-monroe Accessed on February 22, 2011
- Marilyn Monroe. Howstuffworks. http://entertainment. howstuffworks.com/marilyn-monroe.htm Accessed on February 22, 2011
- Marilyn Monroe. Wikipedia. http://en.wikipedia.org/wiki/Marilyn_ Monroe Accessed on February 22, 2011
- Marilyn Monroe Biography. Bio.com. http://www.biography.com/ articles/Marilyn-Monroe-9412123 Accessed on February 22, 2011
- Marilyn Monroe Quotes. Goodreads. http://www.goodreads.com/ author/quotes/82952.Marilyn_Monroe Accessed on February 22, 2011

Edgar Allan Poe
- Edgar Allan Poe. The Edgar Allan Poe Society of Baltimore. http:// www.eapoe.org/ Accessed on October 24, 2011
- Edgar Allan Poe. The Literature Network. http://www.online-literature.com/poe/ Accessed on October 24, 2011
- Edgar Allan Poe. MysteryNet.com. http://www.mysterynet.com/ edgar-allan-poe/ Accessed on October 24, 2011
- Edgar Allan Poe. Poe's Life. Poe Museum. http://www.poemuseum. org/life.php Accessed on October 24, 2011
- Edgar Allan Poe. Wikipedia. http://en.wikipedia.org/wiki/Edgar_ Allan_Poe Accessed on October 24, 2011
- Edgar Allan Poe Quotes. Wikiquote. http://en.wikiquote.org/wiki/ Edgar_Allan_Poe Accessed on October 24, 2011

Eleanor Roosevelt
- Eleanor Roosevelt. "Anna Eleanor Roosevelt." Allida M. Black, Ph.D. The George Washington University. http://www.gwu. edu/~erpapers/abouteleanor/erbiography.cfm Accessed on November 5, 2011
- Eleanor Roosevelt. National First Ladies' Library. http://www. firstladies.org/biographies/firstladies.aspx?biography=33 Accessed on November 5, 2011
- Eleanor Roosevelt. The White House. http://www.whitehouse.gov/ about/first-ladies/eleanorroosevelt Accessed on November 5, 2011
- Eleanor Roosevelt. Wikipedia. http://en.wikipedia.org/wiki/ Eleanor_Roosevelt Accessed on November 5, 2011
- Eleanor Roosevelt Quotes. Wikiquotes. http://en.wikiquote.org/ wiki/Eleanor_Roosevelt Accessed on November 5, 2011

Bertrand Russell
- Bertrand Russell. The Bertrand Russell Society. http://users.drew. edu/jlenz/brs.html Accessed on October 26, 2011
- Bertrand Russell. The Nobel Prize in Literature 1950, Bertrand Russell. http://www.nobelprize.org/nobel_prizes/literature/

laureates/1950/russell-bio.html Accessed on October 26, 2011
- Bertrand Russell. Stanford Encyclopedia of Philosophy. http://plato.stanford.edu/entries/russell/ Accessed on October 26, 2011
- Bertrand Russell. Wikipedia. http://en.wikipedia.org/wiki/Bertrand_Russell Accessed on October 26, 2011
- Bertrand Russell Quotes. The Quotations Page. http://www.quotationspage.com/quotes/Bertrand_Russell Accessed on October 26, 2011
- Bertrand Russell Quotes. Wikiquote. http://en.wikiquote.org/wiki/Bertrand_Russell Accessed on October 26, 2011

Babe Ruth
- Babe Ruth. Babe Ruth Central. http://www.baberuthcentral.com/index.asp Accessed on September 18, 2011
- Babe Ruth. Wikipedia. http://en.wikipedia.org/wiki/Babe_Ruth Accessed on September 18, 2011
- Babe Ruth Biography. http://www.baberuth.com/biography/ Accessed on September 18, 2011
- Babe Ruth Quotes. BrainyQuote. http://www.brainyquote.com/quotes/authors/b/babe_ruth_2.html Accessed on September 18, 2011

William Tecumseh Sherman
- William Tecumseh Sherman. Stewart Sifakis. CivilWarHome.com http://www.civilwarhome.com/sherbio.htm Accessed on October 26, 2011
- William Tecumseh Sherman. US Army Center of Military History. http://www.history.army.mil/books/cg&csa/Sherman-WT.htm Accessed on October 26, 2011
- William Tecumseh Sherman. Virtual Museum of the City of San Francisco. http://www.sfmuseum.org/bio/sherman.html Accessed on October 26, 2011
- William Tecumseh Sherman. Wikipedia. http://en.wikipedia.org/wiki/William_Tecumseh_Sherman Accessed on October 26, 2011
- William Tecumseh Sherman Quotes. Wikiquote. http://en.wikiquote.org/wiki/William_Tecumseh_Sherman Accessed on October 26, 2011

Henry Morton Stanley
- David Livingstone. Wikipedia. http://en.wikipedia.org/wiki/David_Livingstone Accessed on January 16, 2011
- Henry Morton Stanley, 1841-1904. Princeton University. http://libweb5.princeton.edu/visual_materials/maps/websites/africa/stanley/stanley.html Accessed on January 16, 2011
- Henry Morton Stanley. "A good man in Africa?" John Carey. London Times. March 18,2007. http://entertainment.timesonline.co.uk/tol/arts_and_entertainment/books/non-fiction/article1513215.ece

Accessed on February 23, 2011
- Sir Henry Morton Stanley. Classic Encyclopedia. http://www.1911encyclopedia.org/Sir_Henry_Morton_Stanley Accessed on January 16, 2011
- Sir Henry Morton Stanley. "Dr. Livingstone, I presume." http://www.historic-uk.com/HistoryUK/Wales-History/Stanley.htm Accessed on January 16, 2011

Dave Thomas
- Dave Thomas (American Businessman). Wikipedia. http://en.wikipedia.org/wiki/Dave_Thomas_(American_businessman) Accessed on September 13, 2011
- Dave Thomas: Entrepreneur And Founder Of Wendy's. GlobalBX. http://blog.globalbx.com/2008/10/30/dave-thomas-entrepreneur-and-founder-of-wendys/ Accessed on September 13, 2011
- Dave Thomas. "Death of a Burger King." People Magazine. http://www.people.com/people/archive/article/0,,20136225,00.html Accessed on September 13, 2011
- Dave Thomas. Wendys.com. http://www.aboutwendys.com/Our-Company/Dave-s-Legacy/ Accessed on September 13, 2011
- Dave Thomas Quotes and Sayings about Life and Business. StrategicBusinessTeam.com http://www.strategicbusinessteam.com/famous-small-business-quotes/dave-thomas-quotes-and-sayings-about-life-and-business/ Accessed on September 13, 2011

Leo Tolstoy
- Leo Tolstoy. Chesterton, G. D.; Perris, G. H.; Garnett, Edward. University of Virginia. http://etext.lib.virginia.edu/etcbin/toccer-new2?id=CheTols.sgm&images=images/modeng&data=/texts/english/modeng/parsed&tag=public&part=all Accessed on February 2, 2011
- Leo Tolstoy. Leo Finegold. http://www.linguadex.com/tolstoy/introduction.htm Accessed on February 2, 2011
- Leo Tolstoy. The Literature Network. http://www.online-literature.com/tolstoy/ Accessed on February 2, 2011
- Leo Tolstoy. Wikipedia. http://en.wikipedia.org/wiki/Leo_Tolstoy Accessed on February 2, 2011
- Leo Tolstoy Quotes. http://www.brainyquote.com/quotes/authors/l/leo_tolstoy.html Accessed on February 2, 2011

Phillis Wheatley
- Phillis Wheatley. Ann Woodlief. Virginia Commonwealth University http://www.vcu.edu/engweb/webtexts/Wheatley/philbio.htm Accessed on October 24, 2011
- Phillis Wheatley. The Massachusetts Historical Society. http://www.masshist.org/endofslavery/?queryID=57 Accessed on October 24, 2011

- Phillis Wheatley. Paul P. Reuben. Chapter 2 of Perspectives in American Literature - A Research and Reference Guide - An Ongoing Project. http://www.csustan.edu/english/reuben/pal/ chap2/wheatley.html Accessed on October 24, 2011
- Phillis Wheatley. Wikipedia. http://en.wikipedia.org/wiki/Phillis_ Wheatley Accessed on October 24, 2011
- Phillis Wheatley. Women in History. http://www.lkwdpl.org/ wihohio/whea-phi.htm Accessed on October 24, 2011

Malcolm X
- Malcolm X. AfricaWithin.com. http://www.africawithin.com/ malcolmx/malcolm_bio.htm Accessed on October 30, 2011
- Malcolm X. Bio.com. http://www.biography.com/people/malcolm-x-9396195 Accessed on October 30, 2011
- Malcolm X. Malcom-x.org. http://www.malcolm-x.org/ Accessed on October 30, 2011
- Malcolm X. Official Website. http://www.malcolmx.com/ Accessed on October 30, 2011
- Malcolm X. Wikipedia. http://en.wikipedia.org/wiki/Malcolm_X Accessed on October 30, 2011
- Malcolm X Quotes. Wikiquote. http://en.wikiquote.org/wiki/ Malcolm_X Accessed on October 30, 2011

Well-Known People Who Were Adopted

Frances Alda
Jani Allan
Andal
Edward Anderson
Ben Andrews
Maya Angelou
Ann-Margret
Josephine Antoine
Pius Antonius
William Apess
Aristotle
Louis Armstrong
Edith Ashcroft
John Aspinall
Joshua Astor
Kevyn Aucoin
John Audubon
Caesar Augustus
Jimmy Baca
Johann Bach
Oksana Baiul
Josephine Baker
John Ballinger
Tallulah Bankhead
John Banks
Dee Barber
Freddie Bartholomew
John Bartram
Daisy Bates
Jamie Baulch
Michael Bay
James Bayard
Layne Beachley
Ennis Beley
James Bellwood
John Bemo
Sira Ben

David Berglas
Ingrid Bergman
Andy Berlin
Nicole Bilderback
Elizabeth Bishop
Clot Blood
Simón Bolívar
Jim Bowen
William Bradford
John Brady
Dilly Braimoh
David Brainerd
James Brickley
Harold Brodkey
Angie Brooks-Randolph
Pierce Brosnan
James Brown
Leslie Brown
Lester Brown
Thomas Bullock
Andrew Burke
Kathy Burke
Burnum Burnum
Richard Burton
Darcey Bussell
William Bustamante
Robert Byrd
James Caddell
Dean Cain
Michael Caines
John Callahan
Rhona Cameron
Alistair Campbell
Ben Campbell
Truman Capote
Abraham Cardozo
Louis Carl

Richard Carlson
Kev Carmody
Harold Carr
Kitty Carruthers
Peter Carruthers
Forrest Carter
George Washington Carver
Rosemary Casals
Roger Casement
Branco Castelo
Pete Catches
Charles Chaplin
Jean Charbonneau
Horn Chips
Colin Chisholm
Charlotte Church
Eric Clapton
William Clinton
Jacqueline Cochran
Cadwallader Colden
Nat Cole
Brian Connolly
Joseph Conrad
Catherine Cookson
Sherman Coolidge
Patricia Cornwell
Crazy Horse
George Custis
Daniel Davies
Edward Dahlberg
Faith Daniels
Alexandra Danilova
Ted Danson
Alighieri Dante
Tommy Davidson
William Davies
John Davis

Joseph Deacon
James Dean
Paora Delamere
Édouard Dermit
Jeff Diamond
Eric Dickerson
David Dickinson
Bo Diddley
Adrian Dodson
Michael Dodson
Patrick Dodson
Anthony Douglas
Catherine Douglas
Frederick Douglass
Donny Dowd
Carl-Theodor
Dreyer
Peter Duchin
Charles Eastman
Peter Eaton
Edward VI
LonneElder
Edward Ellison
Lawrence Ellison
Louis Emerick
Olaudah Equiano
Erichthonius
Clarissa Estés
Esther
Eumenes
Barry Evans
David Farragut
John Fashanu
Justinius Fashanu
Fred Fever
Shirley Field
Peter Finch
Mac Finn

Laura Fish
Antwone Fisher
Florence Fisher
Ella Fitzgerald
Gerald Ford
Miloš Forman
Percy Fowler
Ruth Fox
Adelaide Foyster
Phil Frampton
Benjamin Francis
Peter Francisco
Eva Frank
Mike Frankovich
Frederick
Frelinghuysen
Olive Fremstad
Marti Friedlander
Victoria Fyodorova
Wira Gardiner
William Garrison
Elizabeth Gaskell
Piers Gaveston
John Gay
Adeline Genée
Jean Genet
Jonathan Gilbert
Melissa Gilbert
Madge Gill
Newton Gingrich
Tom Glazer
Sidney Glazier
Sam Goldwyn
Evonne Goolagong
Clare Gorham
Eddie Graham
Kenneth Grahame
Julia Grant

Larry Grayson
Tim Green
Owl Grey
Joseph Griffis
Calvin Griffith
Roger Grimsby
Ummetüllah Gülnüs
Matthew Hale
Alexander Hamilton
Scott Hamilton
John Hancock
Abram Hannibal
Ashia Hansen
Pakariki Harrison
Deborah Harry
Joseph Haydn
Lemuel Haynes
Bessie Head
Albert Hensley
Matthew Henson
David Hill
Faith Hill
Daisy Hilton
Damien Hirst
Eric Hobsbawm
Ann Holmes
Gary Holt
Herbert Hoover
Antony Hopkins
Harry Houdini
Samuel Houston
Langston Hughes
Joseph Hyde
Orson Hyde
Pasha Ibrahim
Ice-T
Isidore
Tame Iti

Andrew Jackson
Henry Jackson
Jesse Jackson
Thomas Jonathan Jackson
Peter Jacobs
Malcolm Jagamarra
Jakko Jakszyk
Lennie James
Wendy James
Derek Jameson
Zane Jarvis
Robert Jenkins
Steve Jobs
Nkosi Johnson
David Jones
Frederick Jones
Pei Jones
Stewart Jones
Benito Juárez
Sanraku Kano
Sansetsu Kano
Jackie Kay
Edmund Kean
John Keats
Johannes Kepler
Cynthia Kereluk
Rudyard Kipling
Nobusuke Kishi
Eartha Kitt
Edward Knight
Lawrence Kutner
Marr La
Florence LaBadie
Matthew Laborteaux
Patrick Laborteaux
John Langston

Frank Langstone
Jane Lapotaire
Robert Laurent
Frances Lear
George Lee
John Lee
Henry Lehmann
David Leitch
Leslie Lemke
John Lennon
Hugh Leonard
Anna Leonowens
Dilwyn Lewis
Edmonia Lewis
Eleanor Lewis
Peng Li
Alice Liddell
Betty Lifton
Huoping Lin
Art Linkletter
Ray Liotta
Liesbeth List
Richard Little
Sun Little
Gordon Liu
Ellis Lloyd
Delos Lonewolf
Lance Long
Charlotte Lopez
Gregory Louganis
Makere Love
Scott Lowell
David Loxterkamp
Gim Lue
Sarah McLachlan
Edward Mabo
James MacArthur
Wally Macarthur

Roger MacBride
Anna Magnani
Lee Majors
Nelson Mandela
Andrea Mantegna
Eruera Manuera
William Mariner
Harry Martinson
Sophia Mason
Edith Massey
Ivan Massow
Tom Masters
William Maugham
Thabo Mbeki
Catherine McAuley
Mary McCarthy
Thaddeus McCarthy
Heather McCartney
Desmond McDaid
Dylan McDermott
Tim McGraw
Richard McKenzie
Sarah McLachlan
Doris McMillon
Andy McNab
Steve McQueen
Narelle McRobbie
Mike McShane
Michael Medwin
Terry Melcher
Herman Melville
Francesco Melzi
Christopher Memminger
Julius Meyer
James Michener
Plwm Mici
Philip Middlemiss

Dorothy Mihinui
Stan Mikita
Billy Mills
Robert Mills
Keen Mo
Thomas Monaghan
Marilyn Monroe
William Monroe
Carlos Montezuma
Lucy Montgomery
Brian Moore
Luke Morcom
Tukoroirangi
Morgan
John Moriarty
Eric Morley
Neil Morrissey
Edgardo Mortara
Samantha Morton
Moses
Wolf Mountain
Alonzo Mourning
Yoshi Muko
Kaj Munk
Edward Murphy
Andrew Murray
James Mustache
Billie Myers
Paul Myners
James Naismith
Bif Naked
Willie Nelson
John Nettles
Robert Newman
Jack Nicholson
Daniel O Brien
James OConnell
Hugh O Connor

Keishu Okada
Bruce Oldfield
Ngatau Omahuru
Robert ONeil
James Palmer
Tame Parata
Quanah Parker
Lorraine Pascale
Giovanni Pàscoli
Irene Paulger
David Pelzer
Charles Perkins
Caroline Perrott
Elizabeth Phair
Tony Pidgley
Otene Pitau
River Pitt
Dana Plato
Edgar Allan Poe
Sarah Ponsonby
Wiremu Poutapu
Liana Poutu
Peter Powell
Priscilla Presley
Yevgeny Primakov
Robert Pryse
Quetzalcoatl
Katherine Quinn
Phil Quinn
Henry Raeburn
Topsy Ratahi
Raniera Ratana
Tahupotiki Ratana
Michael Reagan
Nancy Reagan
Ebenezer Rees
George Reynolds
Anna Richardson

Wilson Riles
Archie Roach
Harold Robbins
Bill Robinson
Helen Rollason
Eleanor Roosevelt
Tipi Ropiha
Renee Rosnes
Jean-Jacques
Rousseau
Victoria Rowell
Martin Rowson
Bertrand Russel
Kenana Rua
Raharui Rukupo
George Herman
Ruth
Sacagawea
Sarah Saffian
Siro Saigo
Buffy Sainte-Marie
Shane Salter
Samuel
Ignatius Sancho
Teresa Sanderson
Dan Savage
Brenda Schad
Leo Schramm
Lorna Schreiber
Eric Schweig
George Scott
Todd Scott
Julia Scully
Michael Seed
Joe Senser
Alan Seymour
Betty Shabazz
Kenneth Shelton

Fincourt Shelton
Shenandoah
William Tecumseh Sherman
Scott Sherrin
Paull Shin
William Short
Ella Simon
Vishwanath Singh
Lemn Sissay
Frances Slocum
John Smith
Robyn Smith
Venture Smith
Joe Soll
Natsume Soseki
Henry Spalding
Percy Spencer
Albert Stanhope
Henry Morton Stanley
Albert Stewart
Richard Stokes
John Stradling
Barbara Strozzi
Julia Sudbury
Kewang Sun
Jonathan Swift
Annette Sykes
Sonny Taare
Tio Takuta
Mountain Tall
Whangai Tamaiti
Nui Tangiia
Tecumseh
Kateri Tekakwitha
James Templer
Tenskwatawa

Tui Terupe
Dave Thomas
Leslie Thomas
R. Thomas
William Thomas
John Thomson
Grahame Thorne
Giovanni Tiepolo
Sydney Tierney
Hue Tinh
Tito
J.R.R. Tolkien
Leo Tolstoy
Airini Tonore
Joanna Traynor
François Truffaut
Joseph Tydings
Mike Tyson
Maurice Utrillo
Helena Valero
Vanessa-Mae
Mordechai Vanunu
François Villon
Lippvon
Te Waaka
C.J. Walker
Edgar Wallace
Glenyse Ward
Betty Wark
William Waters
Paul Watton
Tumoana Webster
Arnold Weinstock
Bruce Welch
Ruth Westheimer
Te Whaitiri
Phillis Wheatley
Caron Wheeler

Fatima Whitbread
Donald White
Eartha White
Phillip Whitehead
Marcus Whitman
Eliezer Wiesel
Terry Wiles
George Wilkins
Binjamin Wilkomirski
Anthony Williams
Daniel Williams
Jett Williams
John Williams
Flip Wilson
Maria Wine
Oprah Winfrey
Jeanette Winterson
William Wirt
Degaga Wolde
Dorothy Wordsworth
William Wordsworth
Allen Wright
Richard Wright
Malcolm X

Acknowledgements

There are many minds and hands that are involved in any serious writing. I express sincere gratitude to all.

Thank you to my wife, Arlene, for her help, friendship, love, and encouragement.

Thank you to Lonn Litchfield, my law partner and friend of many years, for working with me on so many adoptions and opening my eyes to the beauty and subtleties of the legal and adoption world—together we became a good lawyer.

Thank you to Michael Chabries whose optimisim and vision helped me complete the effort. Thank you to Marci Wahlquist for her editing assistance.

A special thank you for my brother, Claude, whose research, writing, and creative genius got us over and through many obstacles. To my son, John, whose creative talents and dogged tenacity moved us steadily forward. To both, for untiringly listening to my endless ideas and changes.

To all my children who continue to teach me the deeper meaning of love.

A very, very special thank you to my adopted children, without whom I would have never even thought of this book.

Lastly, and most importantly, my deepest gratitude to Him to whom we owe all gratitude.

Gregory P. Hawkins

Greg's legal career spans three decades. As a lawyer he has concentrated much of his professional life weaving a path through the legal labyrinth of adoption—from the most straight-forward adoption to complex litigation—locally, nationally and internationally.

Greg is also a father with a large and expanding family, including four adopted children, grandchildren and the continuing addition of sons and daughters-in-law.

He currently resides in Salt Lake City, Utah, with his wife, Arlene. He continues to write, practice law and promote good public policy.

Someday he hopes to become well acquainted with a fishing pole.

CPSIA information can be obtained at www.ICGtesting.com
Printed in the USA
LVOW080555031012

301163LV00004B/42/P